AN ATLAS OF PLANT STRUCTURE: VOLUME 1

by W. H. Freeman and Brian Bracegirdle

An Atlas of Invertebrate Structure
An Atlas of Embryology
An Atlas of Histology

by Brian Bracegirdle and Patricia H. Miles

An Atlas of Plant Structure: Volume 1
An Atlas of Plant Structure: Volume 2
An Atlas of Chordate Structure

AN ATLAS OF

Plant Structure

Volume 1

Brian Bracegirdle *BSc PhD FIBiol FRPS*

Patricia H Miles *MSc MIBiol ARPS*

Heinemann Educational Books
London

Heinemann Educational Books Ltd
22 Bedford Square, London WC1B 3HH

London Edinburgh Melbourne Auckland
Hong Kong Singapore Kuala Lumpur New Delhi
Ibadan Nairobi Johannesburg
Portsmouth (NH) Kingston Port of Spain

ISBN 0 435 60312 4

Printed in Great Britain by
Fletcher & Son Ltd, Norwich and bound by
Richard Clay (The Chaucer Press) Ltd, Bungay, Suffolk

Preface

This book is designed to be used in the laboratory, to help the student interpret his own material. The contents have been selected to be useful at 'A'-level and in introductory degree courses; a second volume is in active preparation to extend the range of specimens covered.

We have followed the now well-established plan of facing photographs with interpretive line-drawings. All the photographs have been made specially for this book and every effort has been made to retain the detail which the student will see on his slides. The drawings have been made entirely independently of the photographs, with all the advantages of change of focus and magnification that this implies.

The material used for the book has been of good quality and our own collections have been most generously augmented by the Examination Laboratories of the University of London; Philip Harris Biological Supplies Ltd; and The Polytechnic of Central London. To our friends in these places we are sincerely indebted.

Mr John Haller of Philip Harris Biological Supplies Ltd has been a tower of strength. His own excellent collection of slides has been placed at our disposal and in addition his sage advice has been invaluable in deciding contents and obtaining unusual material when it was needed. Indeed, the original impetus for an atlas of plant structure, to match others on animal material, came from Mr Haller.

John Juniper and Clive Wyborn, our readers, have saved us from a number of errors and have been enthusiastic in their support for the project right from the time of deciding the original contents list. We owe them much gratitude and hope they have enjoyed their side of the work as we have ours.

1971

B. B.
P. H. M.

11417

COLOUR TRANSPARENCIES FOR PROJECTION

Every picture in this book is available as a 2 × 2 colour slide for projection from *Philip Harris Biological Supplies Ltd, Oldmixon, Weston-super-Mare, Avon.*

The original master transparencies were made at the same time as the negatives for the pictures in this book, exclusively for this company. The authors recommend these slides for their quality and moderate cost as excellent aids to the teaching of plant structure especially in conjunction with this book.

Contents

AN ATLAS OF
Plant Structure
Volume 1

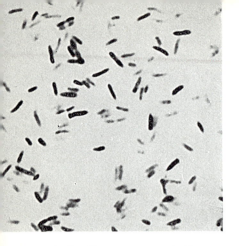

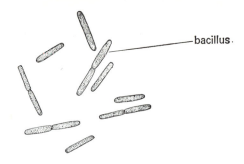

Drawing of part of specimen 1

1. **Bacillus,** separate rods, E.
   Mag. ×2100.

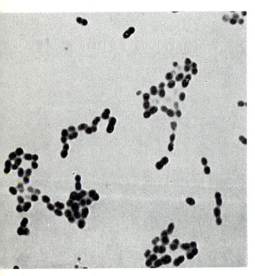

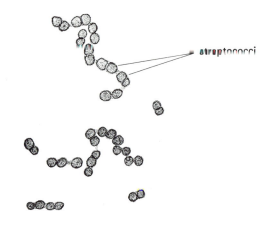

Drawing of part of specimen 2

2. **Coccus,** chains, E. Mag. ×1700.

3. **Spirillum,** E. Mag. ×1400.

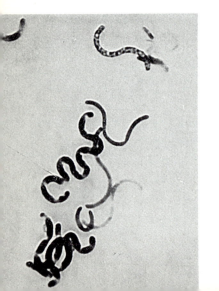

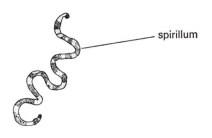

Drawing of part of specimen 3

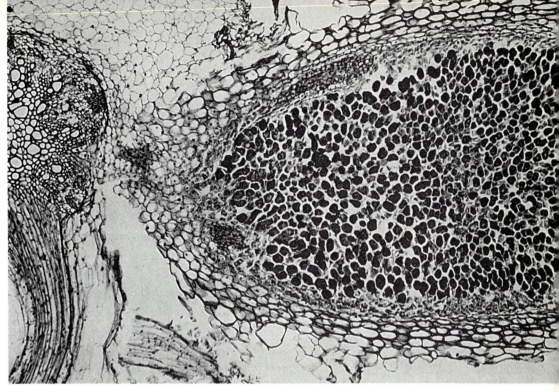

4. **Root nodule of legume,** TS. Mag. ×85.

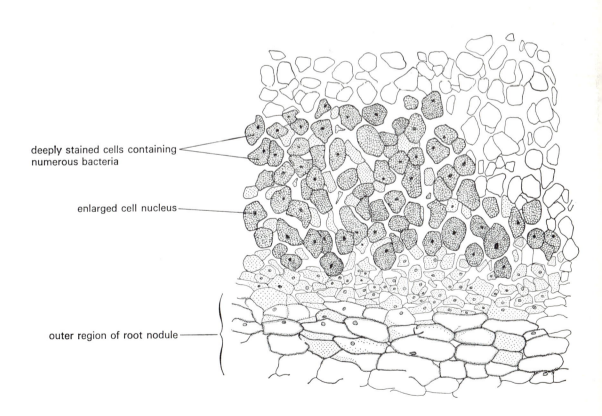

deeply stained cells containing
numerous bacteria

enlarged cell nucleus

outer region of root nodule

Drawing of part of specimen 4

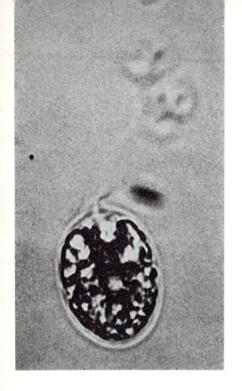

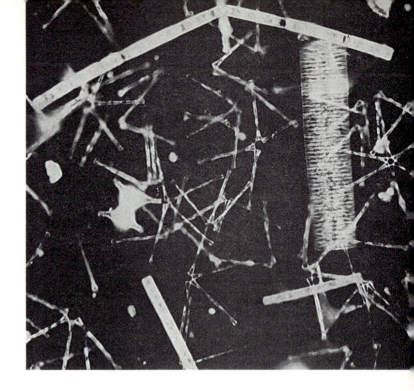

5. **Chlamydomonas**, E, living,
phase contrast. Mag. ×1200

6. **Phytoplankton**, E, strewn slide, dark field. Mag. ×450

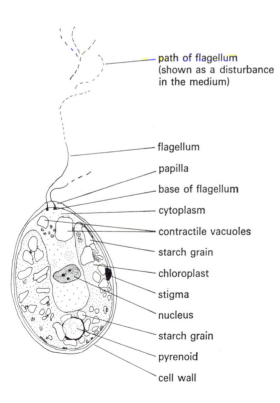

path of flagellum
(shown as a disturbance
in the medium)

flagellum

papilla

base of flagellum

cytoplasm

contractile vacuoles

starch grain

chloroplast

stigma

nucleus

starch grain

pyrenoid

cell wall

Drawing of specimen 5

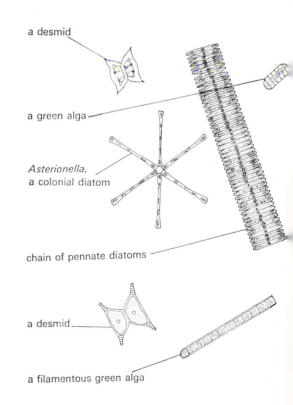

a desmid

a green alga

Asterionella,
a colonial diatom

chain of pennate diatoms

a desmid

a filamentous green alga

Drawing of parts of Specimen

4

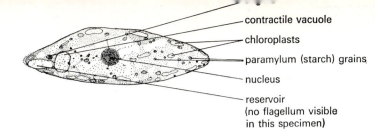

- contractile vacuole
- chloroplasts
- paramylum (starch) grains
- nucleus
- reservoir
  (no flagellum visible
  in this specimen)

7. *Euglena,* E. Mag. ×1050

Drawing of Specimen 7

8. *Volvox,* E, with daughter colonies.
Mag. ×700

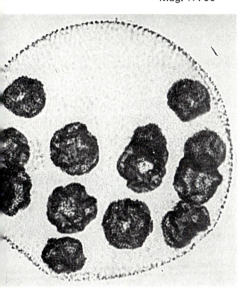

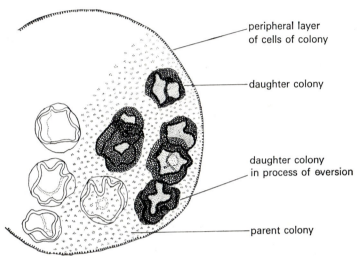

- peripheral layer
  of cells of colony

- daughter colony

- daughter colony
  in process of eversion

- parent colony

Drawing of part of Specimen 8

9. *Volvox,* living, E, surface detail,
phase contrast. Mag. ×1000

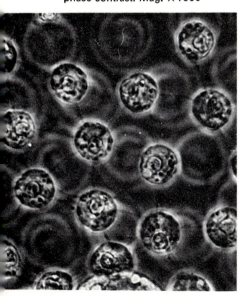

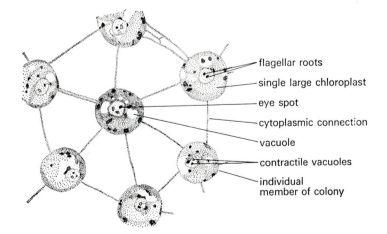

- flagellar roots
- single large chloroplast
- eye spot
- cytoplasmic connection
- vacuole
- contractile vacuoles
- individual
  member of colony

Drawing of Specimen 9

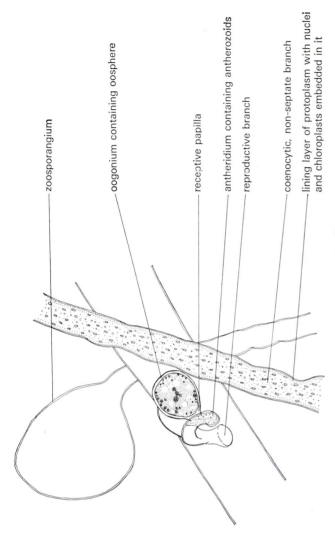

zoosporangium

oogonium containing oosphere

receptive papilla

antheridium containing antherozoids

reproductive branch

coenocytic, non-septate branch

lining layer of protoplasm with nuclei
and chloroplasts embedded in it

Drawing of Specimen 10

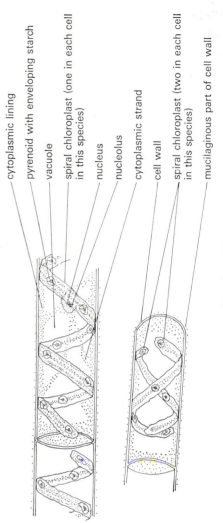

cytoplasmic lining

pyrenoid with enveloping starch

vacuole

spiral chloroplast (one in each cell
in this species)

nucleus

nucleolus

cytoplasmic strand

cell wall

spiral chloroplast (two in each cell
in this species)

mucilaginous part of cell wall

Drawing of Specimen 11

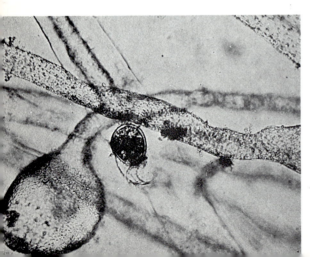

10. *Vaucheria*, living, E. Mag. ×150

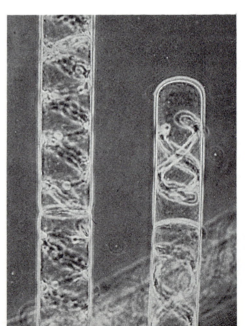

11. *Spirogyra*, living, E, vegetative, phase contrast.
Mag. ×750

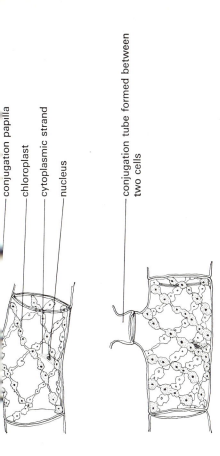

conjugation papilla

chloroplast

cytoplasmic strand

nucleus

conjugation tube formed between two cells

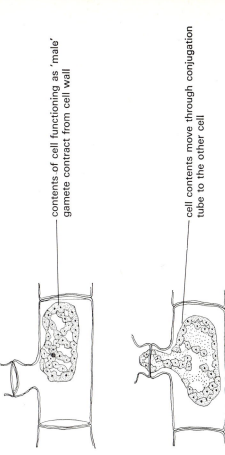

contents of cell functioning as 'male' gamete contract from cell wall

cell contents move through conjugation tube to the other cell

cell contents fuse prior to formation of zygospore

thick wall

gamete nuclei before fusion

Drawings based on Specimen 12

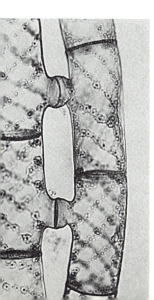

12a. *Spirogyra*, E, conjugation tubes. Mag. × 550

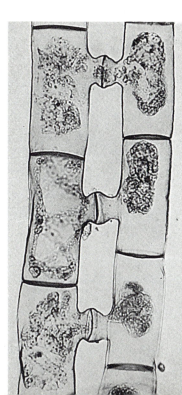

12b. *Spirogyra*, E, migration of 'male' cell contents. Mag. × 550

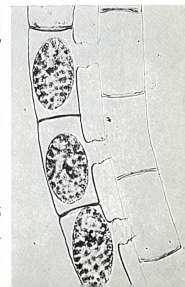

12c. *Spirogyra*, E, union of cell contents. Mag. × 550

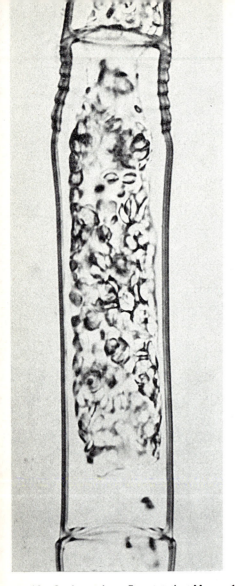

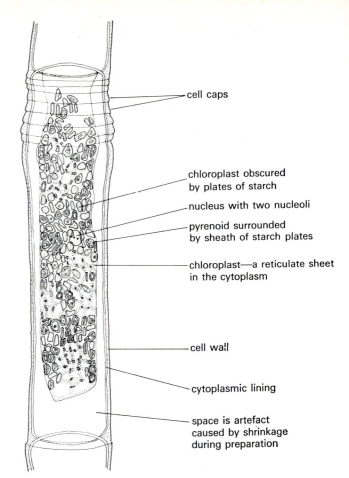

cell caps

chloroplast obscured
by plates of starch

nucleus with two nucleoli

pyrenoid surrounded
by sheath of starch plates

chloroplast—a reticulate sheet
in the cytoplasm

cell wall

cytoplasmic lining

space is artefact
caused by shrinkage
during preparation

Drawing of Specimen 13

13. *Oedogonium*, E, vegetative. Mag. ×150

14. *Oedogonium*, E, reproduction,
dwarf male. Mag. ×65

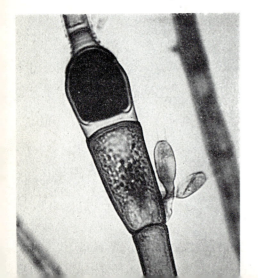

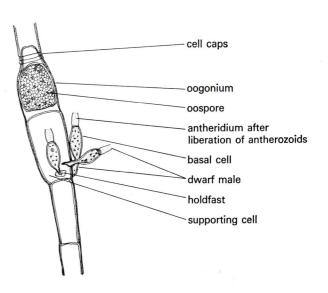

cell caps

oogonium

oospore

antheridium after
liberation of antherozoids

basal cell

dwarf male

holdfast

supporting cell

Drawing of Specimen 14

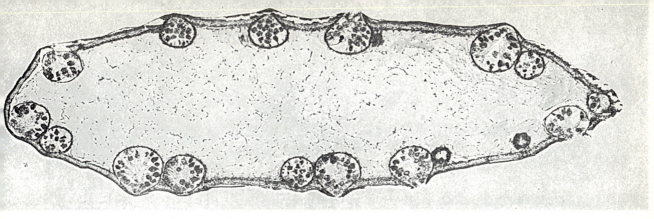

15. *Fucus,* thallus, TS. Mag. ×10

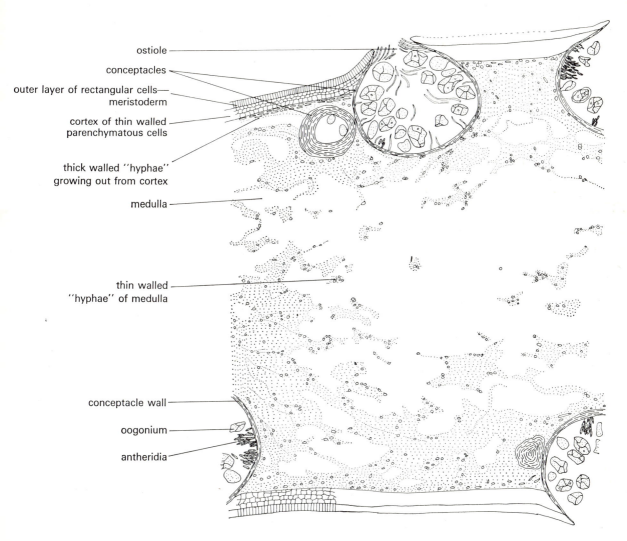

ostiole

conceptacles

outer layer of rectangular cells—
meristoderm

cortex of thin walled
parenchymatous cells

thick walled "hyphae"
growing out from cortex

medulla

thin walled
"hyphae" of medulla

conceptacle wall

oogonium

antheridia

Drawing of part of Specimen 15

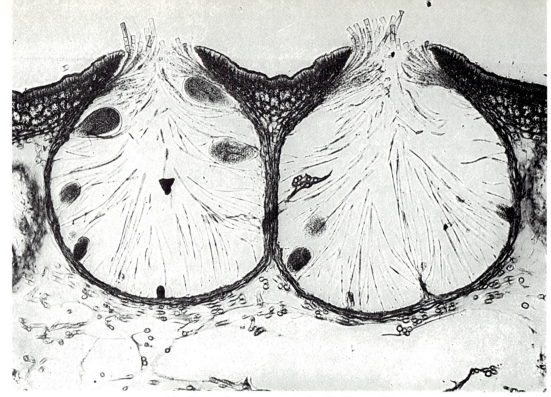

16. *Fucus*, female conceptacle, TS. Mag. ×75

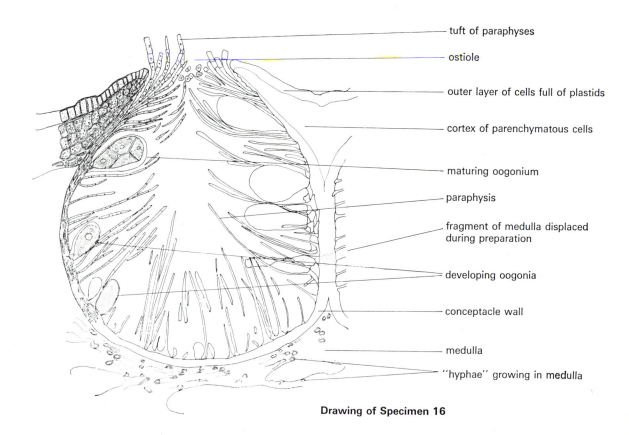

tuft of paraphyses

ostiole

outer layer of cells full of plastids

cortex of parenchymatous cells

maturing oogonium

paraphysis

fragment of medulla displaced during preparation

developing oogonia

conceptacle wall

medulla

"hyphae" growing in medulla

Drawing of Specimen 16

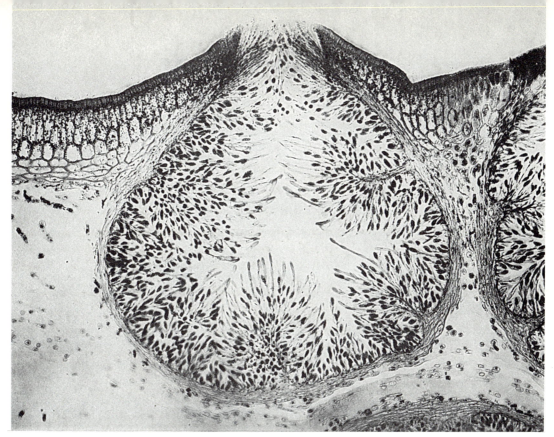

17. *Fucus*, male conceptacle, TS. Mag. ×85

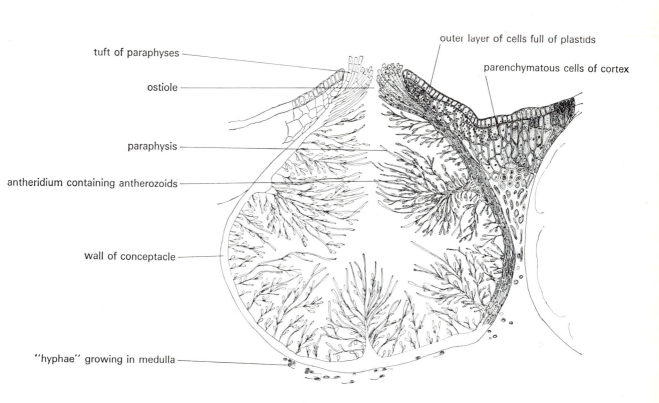

tuft of paraphyses

ostiole

paraphysis

antheridium containing antherozoids

wall of conceptacle

"hyphae" growing in medulla

outer layer of cells full of plastids

parenchymatous cells of cortex

Drawing of Specimen 17

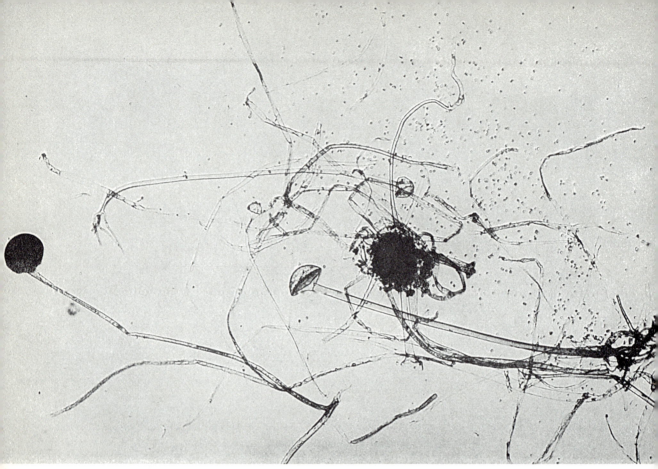

18. *Mucor*, hyphae and sporangia, E. Mag. ×100

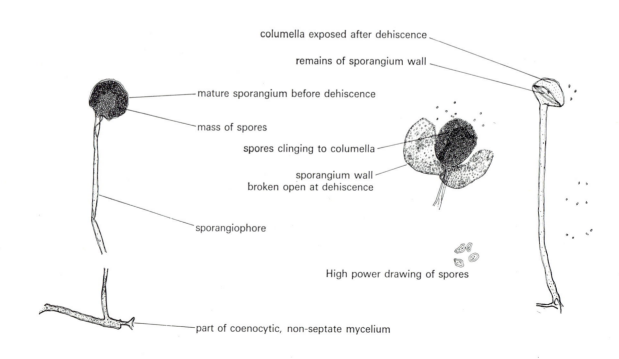

columella exposed after dehiscence

remains of sporangium wall

mature sporangium before dehiscence

mass of spores

spores clinging to columella

sporangium wall
broken open at dehiscence

sporangiophore

High power drawing of spores

part of coenocytic, non-septate mycelium

Drawing of parts of Specimen 18

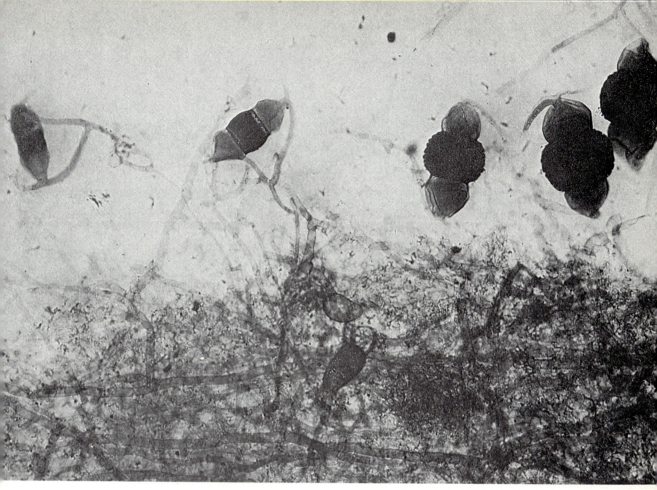

19. **Mucor,** stages in sexual reproduction, E. Mag. ×125

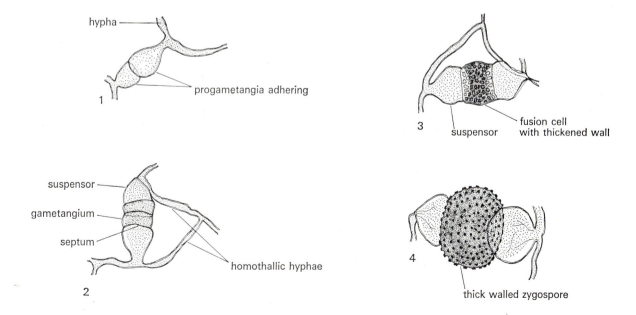

hypha

progametangia adhering

1

suspensor

gametangium

septum

homothallic hyphae

2

3

suspensor

fusion cell
with thickened wall

4

thick walled zygospore

Drawing of parts of Specimen 19

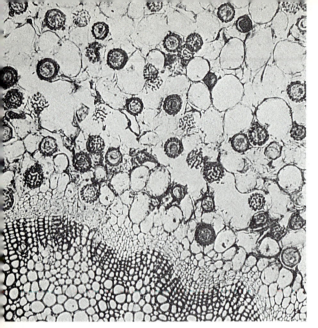

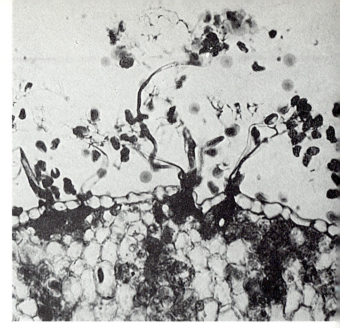

20. **_Cystopus_**, sexual reproduction—oospores TS. Mag. ×150

21. **_Peronospora_**, asexual reproduction and haustoria, TS. Mag. ×175

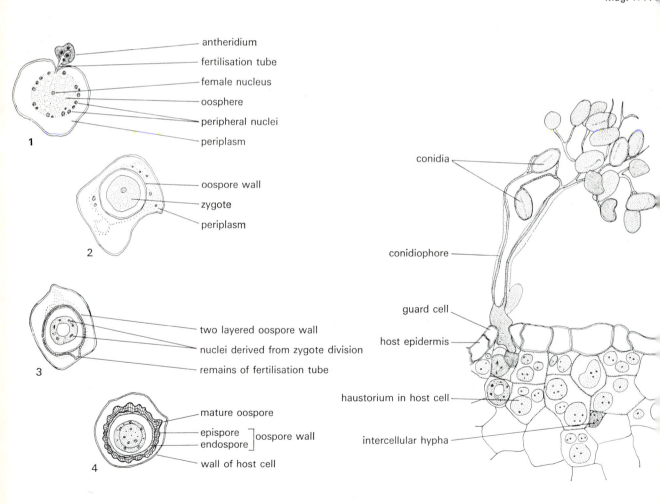

1
- antheridium
- fertilisation tube
- female nucleus
- oosphere
- peripheral nuclei
- periplasm

2
- oospore wall
- zygote
- periplasm

3
- two layered oospore wall
- nuclei derived from zygote division
- remains of fertilisation tube

4
- mature oospore
- epispore ⎤ oospore wall
- endospore ⎦
- wall of host cell

Drawing based on Specimen 20

- conidia
- conidiophore
- guard cell
- host epidermis
- haustorium in host cell
- intercellular hypha

Drawing of Specimen 21

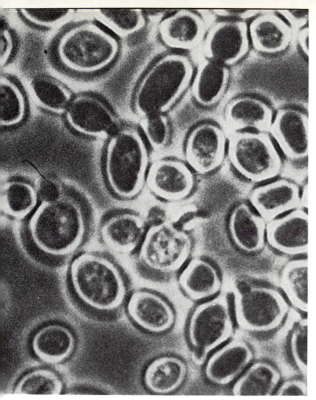

22. *Saccharomyces*, E, budding, living, phase contrast.
Mag. ×900

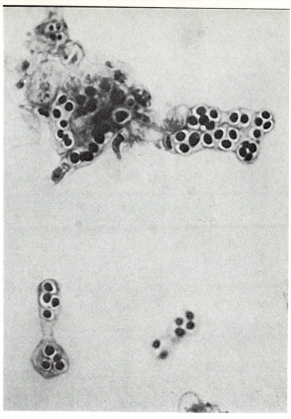

23. *Schizosaccharomyces*, E. Mag. ×1250

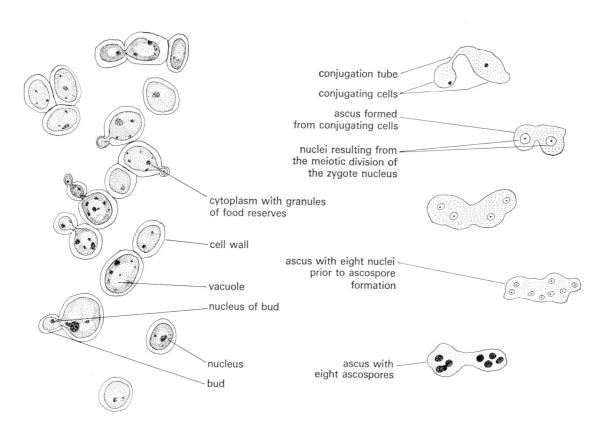

conjugation tube

conjugating cells

ascus formed
from conjugating cells

nuclei resulting from
the meiotic division of
the zygote nucleus

cytoplasm with granules
of food reserves

cell wall

ascus with eight nuclei
prior to ascospore
formation

vacuole

nucleus of bud

nucleus

ascus with
eight ascospores

bud

Drawing of Specimen 22   **Drawings based on Specimen 23**

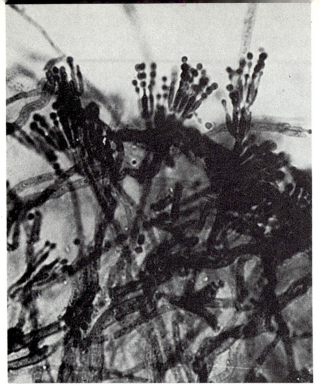

24. **Penicillium,** conidiophores, E. Mag. ×600

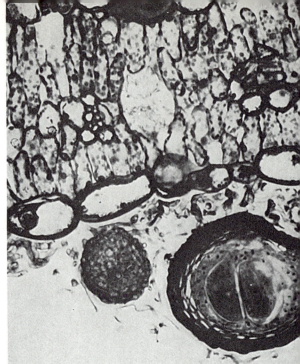

25. **Erysiphe,** cleistothecia and haustoria, TS. Mag. ×400

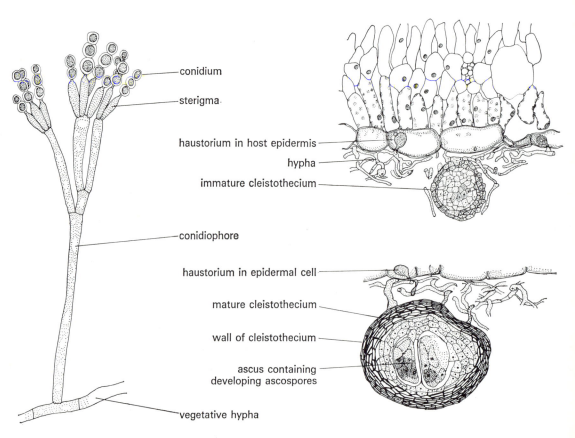

conidium

sterigma

haustorium in host epidermis

hypha

immature cleistothecium

conidiophore

haustorium in epidermal cell

mature cleistothecium

wall of cleistothecium

ascus containing
developing ascospores

vegetative hypha

Drawing of part of Specimen 24

Drawings of Specimen 25

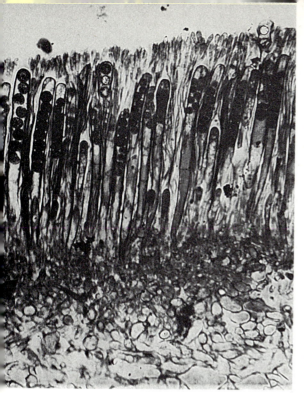

26. **Peziza,** hymenium with asci, VS. Mag. ×750

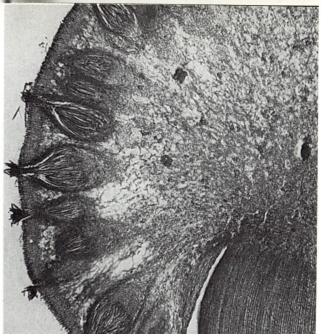

27. **Claviceps,** perithecia, VS. Mag. ×65

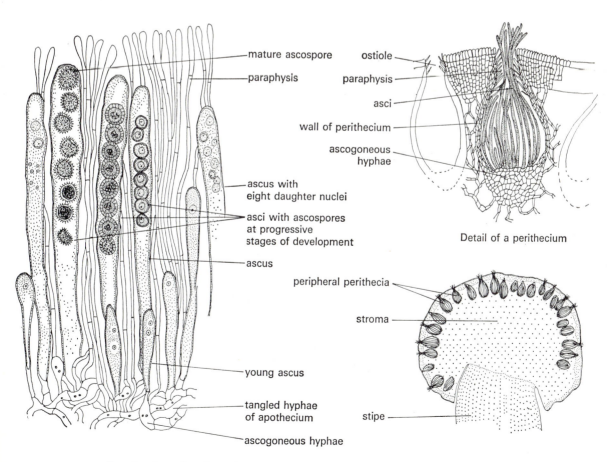

mature ascospore

paraphysis

ascus with
eight daughter nuclei

asci with ascospores
at progressive
stages of development

ascus

young ascus

tangled hyphae
of apothecium

ascogoneous hyphae

ostiole

paraphysis

asci

wall of perithecium

ascogoneous
hyphae

Detail of a perithecium

peripheral perithecia

stroma

stipe

17   **Drawing from Specimen 26**   **Drawings from Specimen 27**

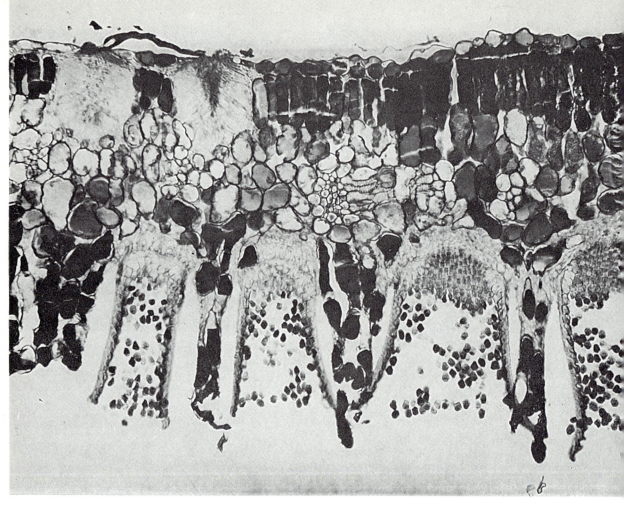

28. *Puccinia*, aecidia and pycnidia, VS. Mag. ×150

29. *Puccinia*, teleutosori, VS. Mag. ×300

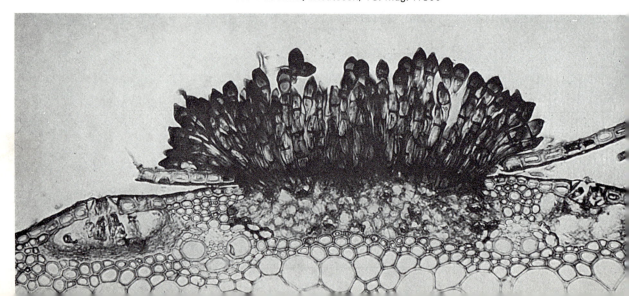

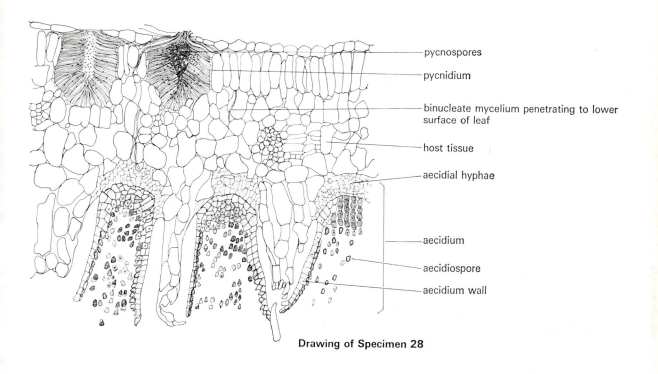

pycnospores

pycnidium

binucleate mycelium penetrating to lower surface of leaf

host tissue

aecidial hyphae

aecidium

aecidiospore

aecidium wall

Drawing of Specimen 28

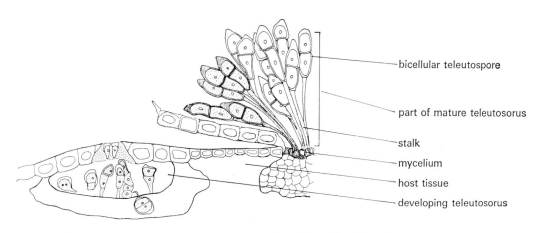

bicellular teleutospore

part of mature teleutosorus

stalk

mycelium

host tissue

developing teleutosorus

Drawing of Specimen 29

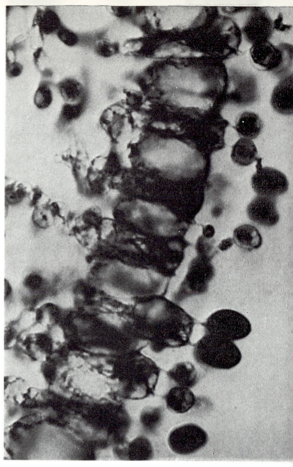

30. **Psalliota**, fruiting body, gross, E. Mag. ×3

31. **Coprinus**, gill basidia, TS. Mag. ×1500

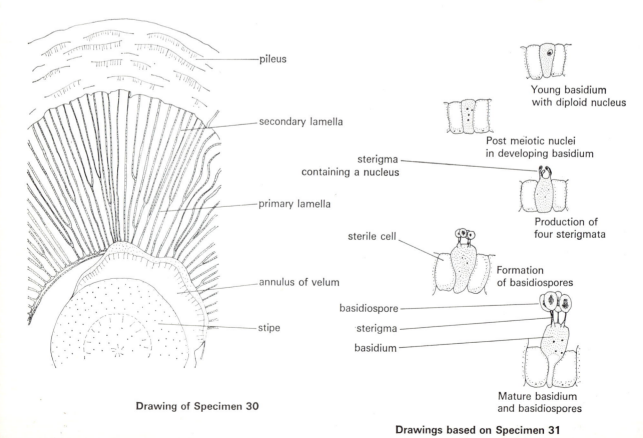

pileus

secondary lamella

sterigma
containing a nucleus

primary lamella

sterile cell

annulus of velum

basidiospore

sterigma

stipe

basidium

Young basidium
with diploid nucleus

Post meiotic nuclei
in developing basidium

Production of
four sterigmata

Formation
of basidiospores

Mature basidium
and basidiospores

Drawing of Specimen 30

Drawings based on Specimen 31

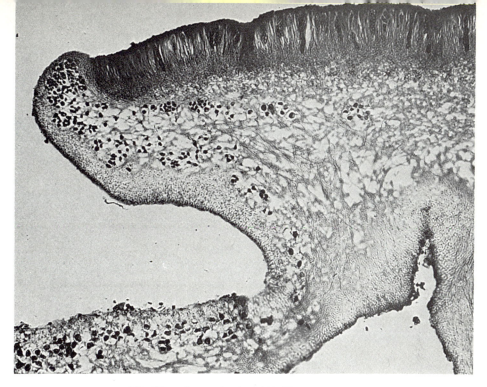

32. *Physcia*, apothecium, VS. Mag. ×110

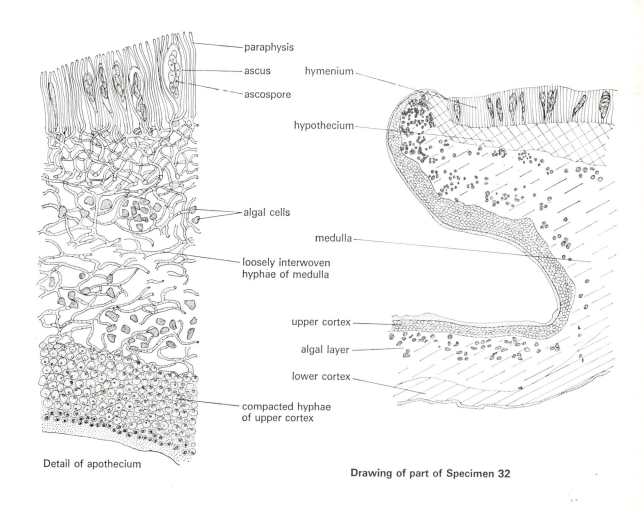

paraphysis

ascus

ascospore

hymenium

hypothecium

algal cells

medulla

loosely interwoven
hyphae of medulla

upper cortex

algal layer

lower cortex

compacted hyphae
of upper cortex

Detail of apothecium

Drawing of part of Specimen 32

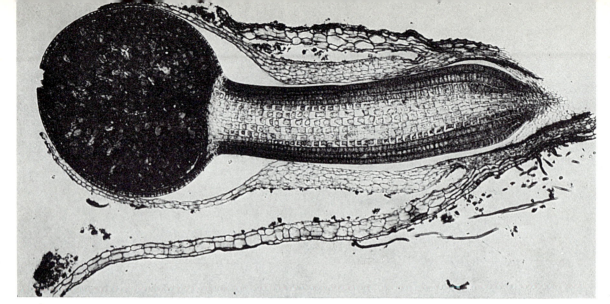

35. *Pellia,* sporangium, LS. Mag. ×55

33. *Pellia,* antheridium, LS. Mag. ×75   34. *Pellia,* archegonium, LS. Mag. ×200

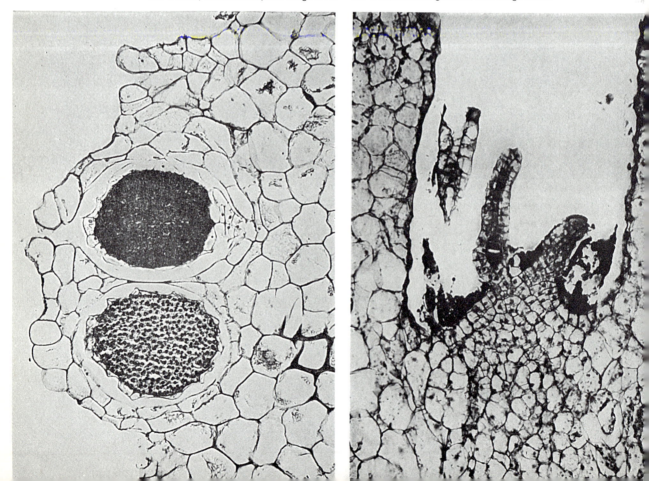

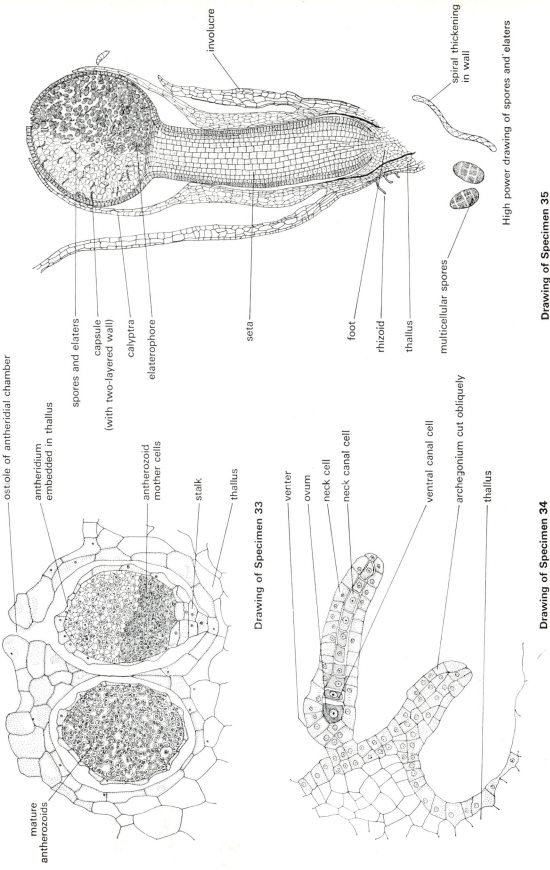

involucre

spiral thickening
in wall

High power drawing of spores and elaters

spores and elaters

capsule
(with two-layered wall)

calyptra

elaterophore

seta

foot

rhizoid

thallus

multicellular spores

Drawing of Specimen 35

ostiole of antheridial chamber

antheridium
embedded in thallus

antherozoid
mother cells

stalk

thallus

mature
antherozoids

Drawing of Specimen 33

venter

ovum

neck cell

neck canal cell

ventral canal cell

archegonium cut obliquely

thallus

Drawing of Specimen 34

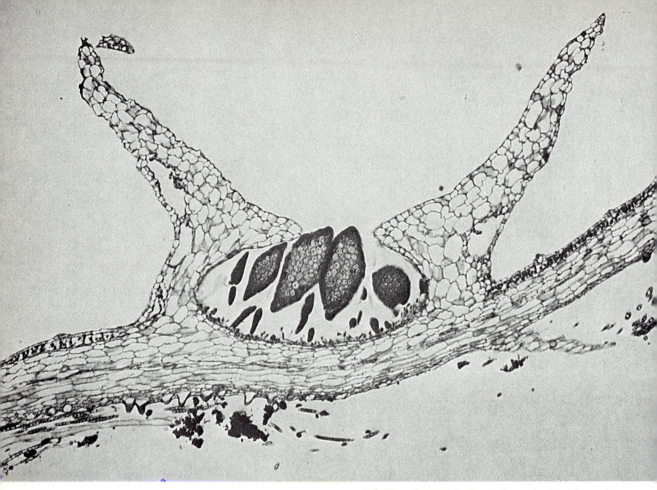

36. *Marchantia,* thallus and cupule, TS. Mag. ×80

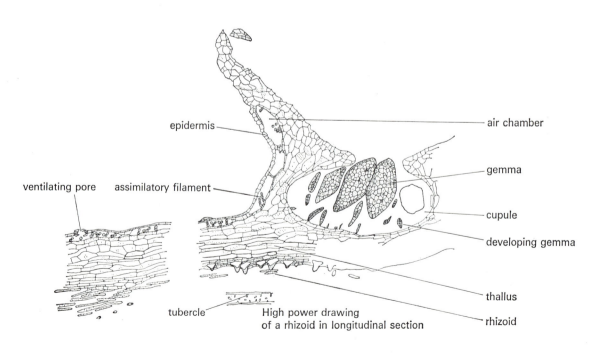

epidermis — air chamber

ventilating pore   assimilatory filament — gemma

cupule

developing gemma

thallus

tubercle   High power drawing   rhizoid
of a rhizoid in longitudinal section

Drawing of Specimen 36

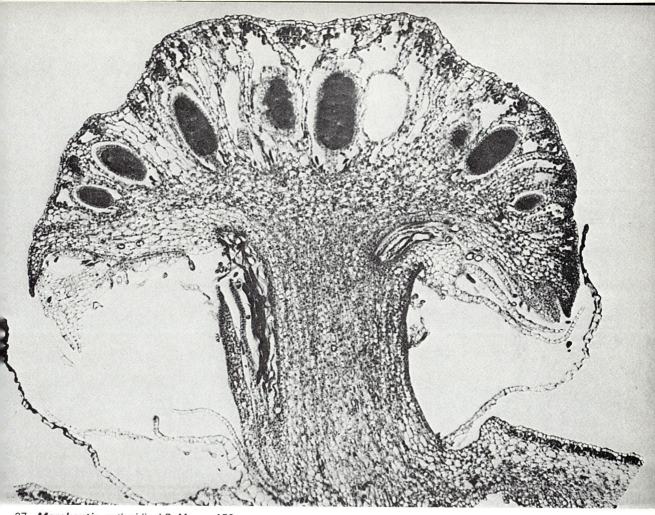

37. *Marchantia,* antheridia, LS. Mag. ×150

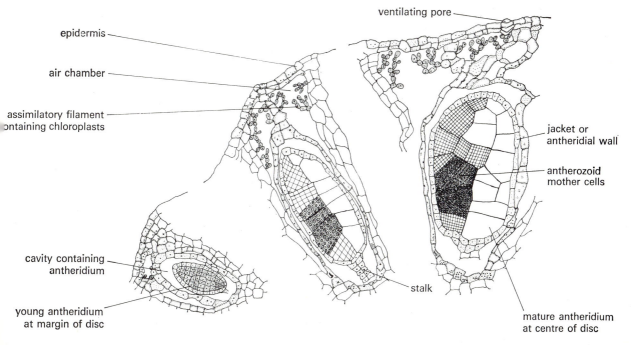

epidermis

air chamber

assimilatory filament
containing chloroplasts

ventilating pore

jacket or
antheridial wall

antherozoid
mother cells

cavity containing
antheridium

young antheridium
at margin of disc

stalk

mature antheridium
at centre of disc

Drawing of parts of Specimen 37

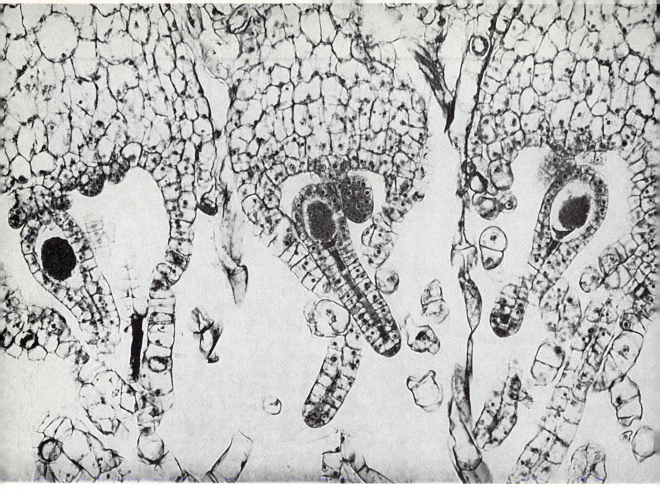

38. *Marchantia,* archegonia, LS. Mag. ×300

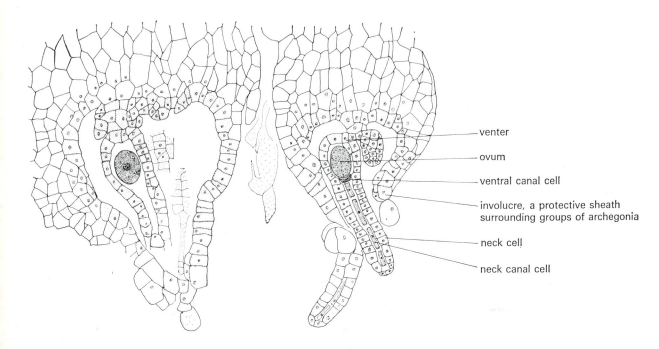

venter

ovum

ventral canal cell

involucre, a protective sheath surrounding groups of archegonia

neck cell

neck canal cell

Drawing of Specimen 38

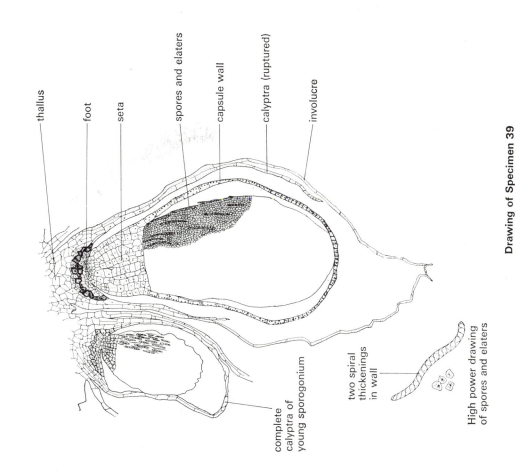

thallus

foot

seta

spores and elaters

capsule wall

calyptra (ruptured)

involucre

complete
calyptra of
young sporogonium

two spiral
thickenings
in wall

High power drawing
of spores and elaters

Drawing of Specimen 39

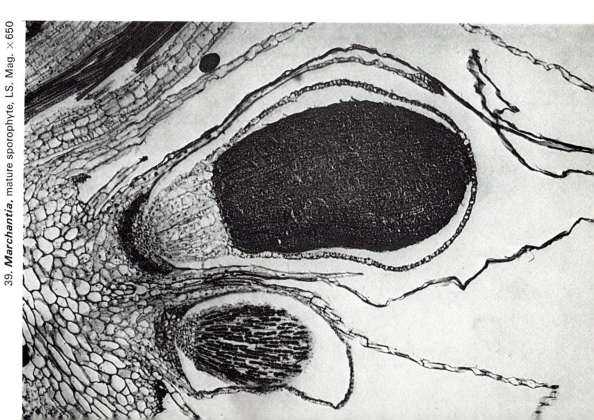

39. *Marchantia,* mature sporophyte, LS. Mag. × 650

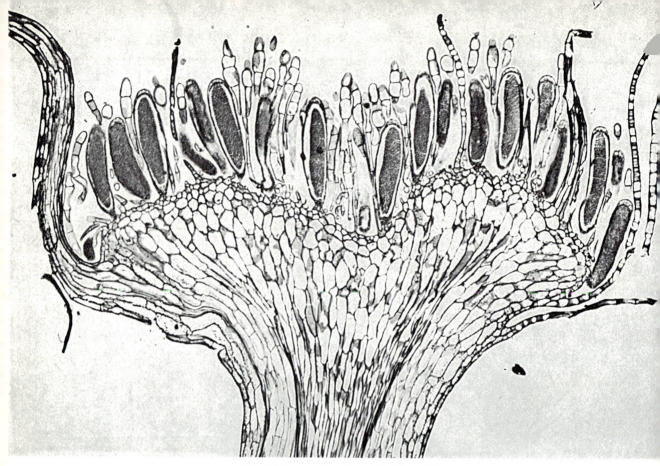

40. **Mnium,** antheridium, LS. Mag. ×90

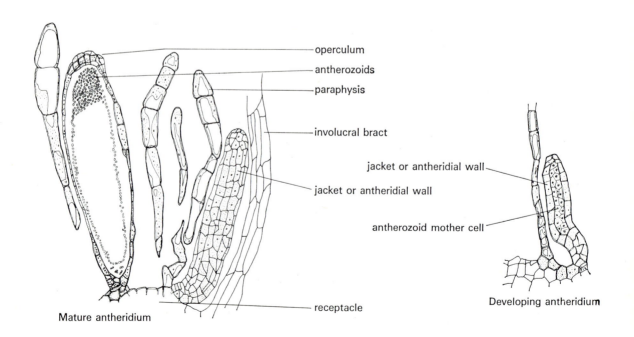

operculum
antherozoids
paraphysis

involucral bract

jacket or antheridial wall

jacket or antheridial wall

antherozoid mother cell

receptacle

Mature antheridium

Developing antheridium

Drawing of part of Specimen 40

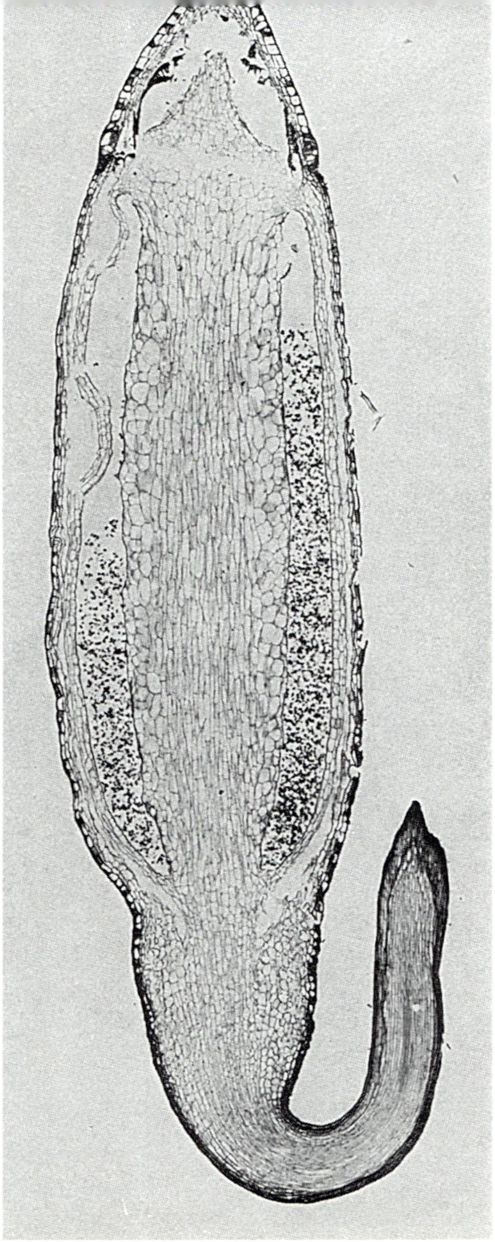

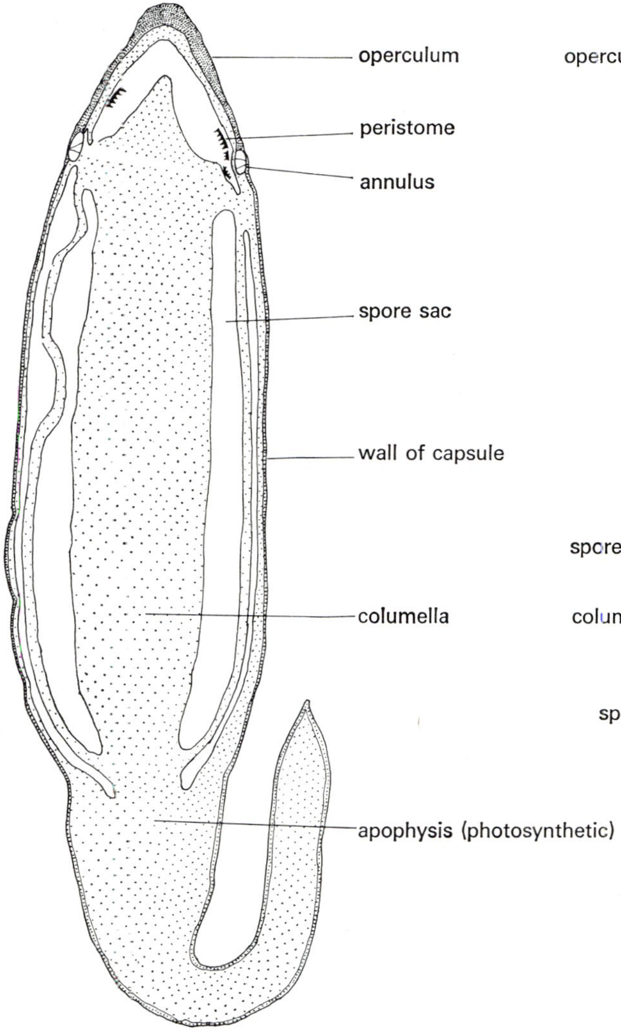

Detail of Specimen 43

peristome teeth
annulus
rim

operculum

spore sac

columella

spores

High power view
of individual spores

operculum

peristome

annulus

spore sac

wall of capsule

columella

apophysis (photosynthetic)

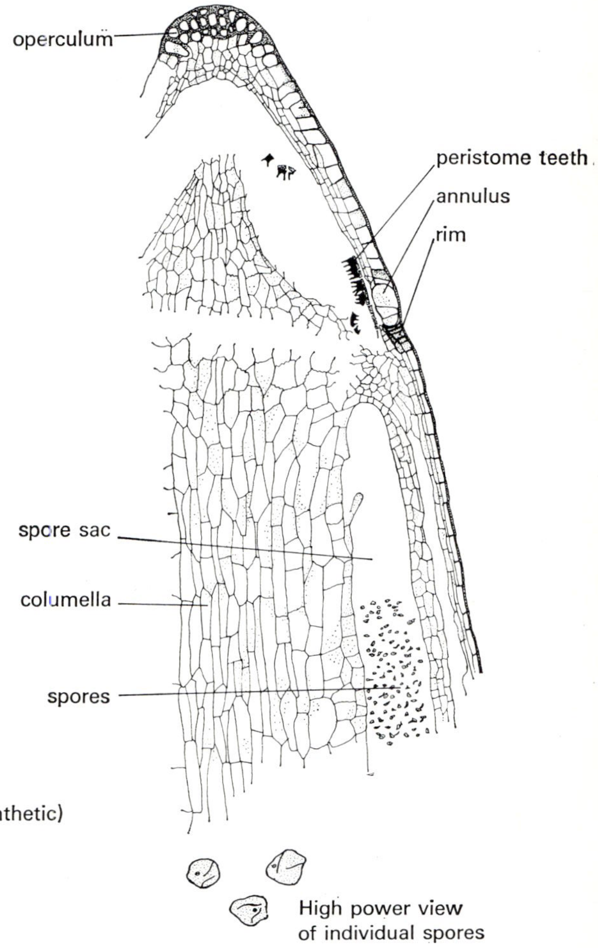

43. _Mnium_, capsule, LS. Mag. ×55

Drawing of Specimen 43

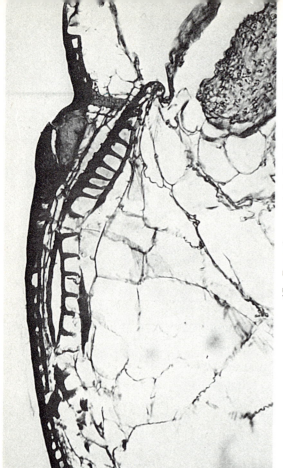

45. *Funaria,* capsule teeth, LS. Mag. ×650

46. *Funaria,* peristome, gross, E. Mag. ×12

44. *Funaria,* capsule, LS. Mag. ×60

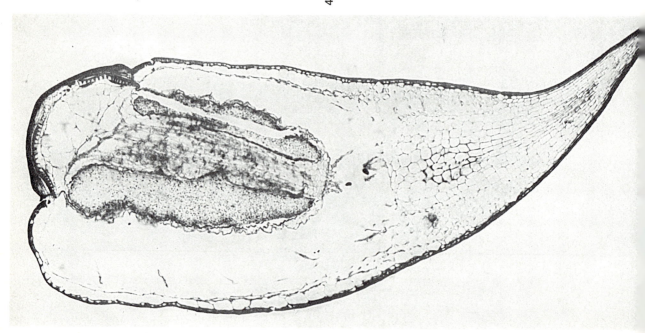

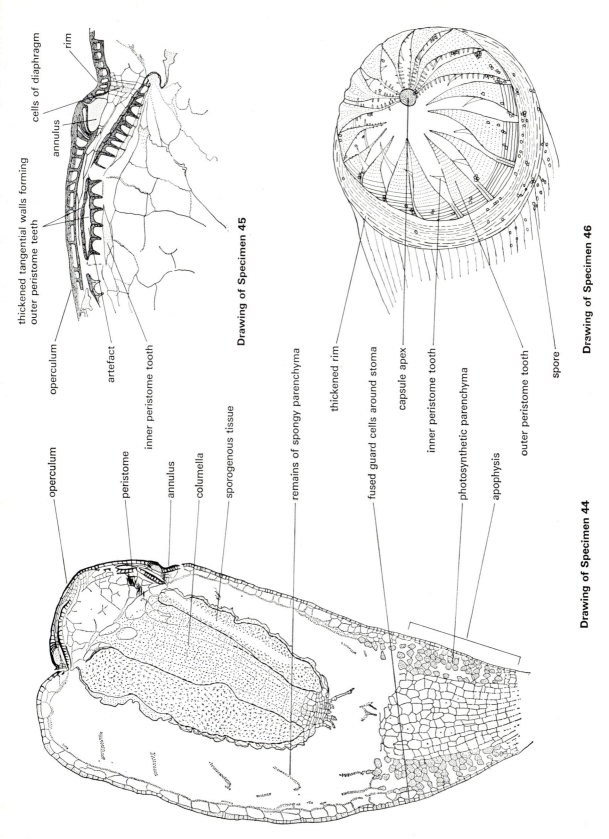

thickened tangential walls forming
outer peristome teeth

cells of diaphragm

rim

annulus

operculum

artefact

inner peristome tooth

Drawing of Specimen 45

operculum

peristome

annulus

columella

sporogenous tissue

remains of spongy parenchyma

thickened rim

fused guard cells around stoma

capsule apex

inner peristome tooth

photosynthetic parenchyma

apophysis

outer peristome tooth

spore

Drawing of Specimen 46

Drawing of Specimen 44

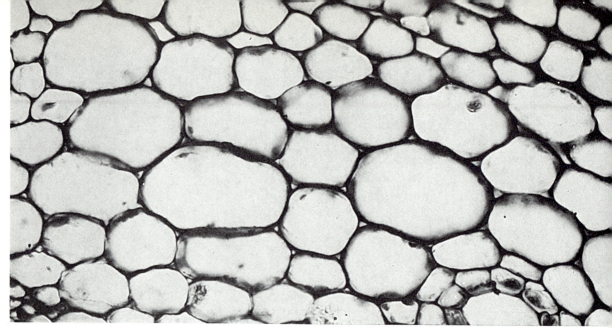

47. **Parenchyma,** TS, from *Helianthus* stem.
Mag. ×300

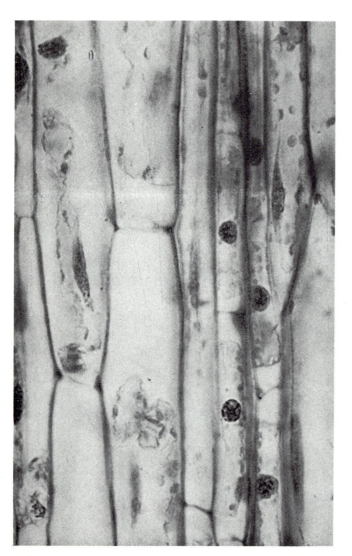

48. **Parenchyma,** LS, from *Helianthus* stem.
Mag. ×300

34

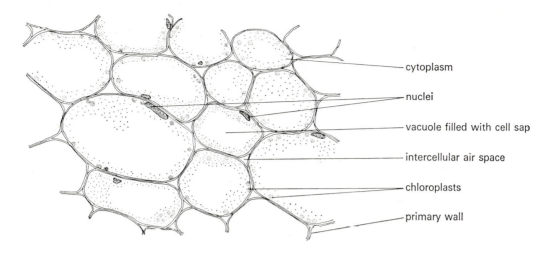

— cytoplasm

— nuclei

— vacuole filled with cell sap

— intercellular air space

— chloroplasts

— primary wall

Drawing of Specimen 47

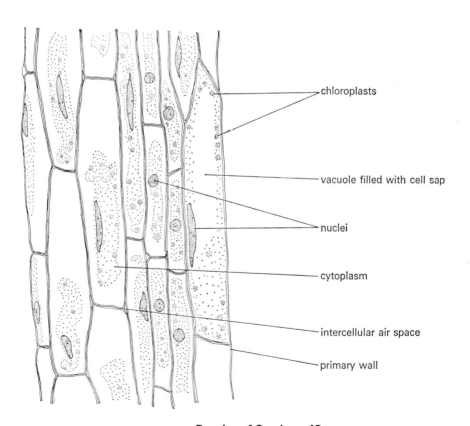

chloroplasts

vacuole filled with cell sap

nuclei

cytoplasm

intercellular air space

primary wall

Drawing of Specimen 48

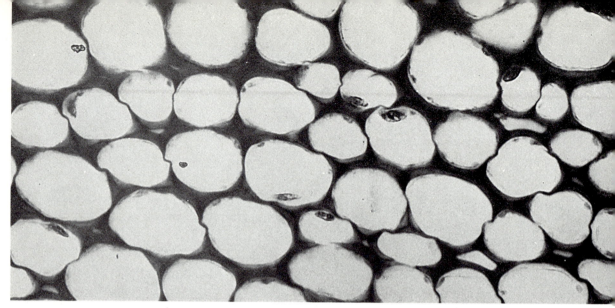

49. **Collenchyma,** TS, from *Helianthus* stem. Mag. ×450

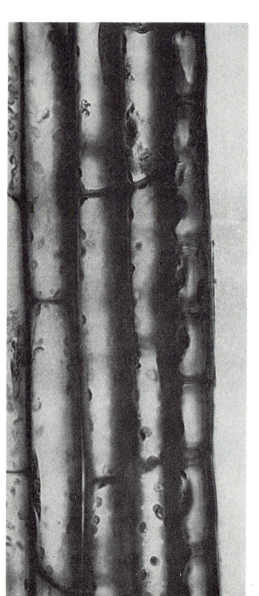

50. **Collenchyma,** LS, from *Helianthus* stem. Mag. ×300

36

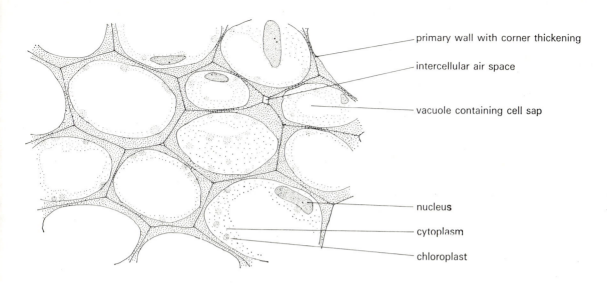

primary wall with corner thickening

intercellular air space

vacuole containing cell sap

nucleus

cytoplasm

chloroplast

Drawing of Specimen 49

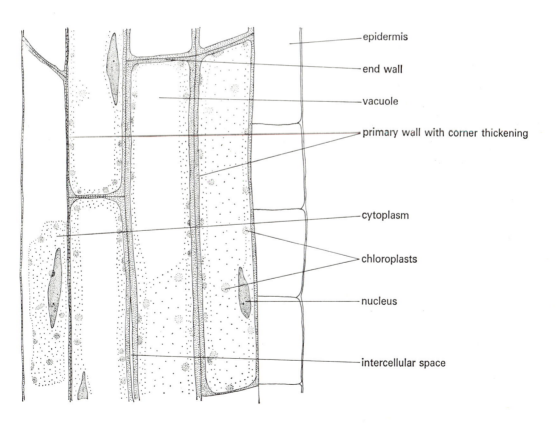

epidermis

end wall

vacuole

primary wall with corner thickening

cytoplasm

chloroplasts

nucleus

intercellular space

Drawing of Specimen 50

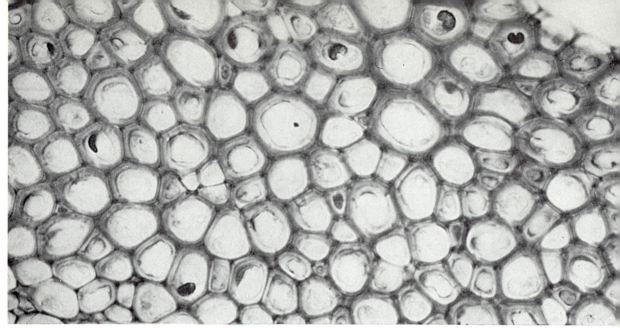

51. **Sclerenchyma,** TS, from *Helianthus* stem. Mag. ×600

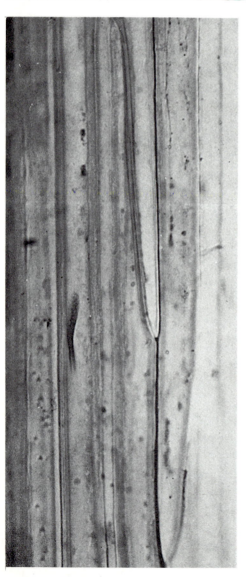

52. **Sclerenchyma,** LS, from *Helianthus* stem. Mag. ×700

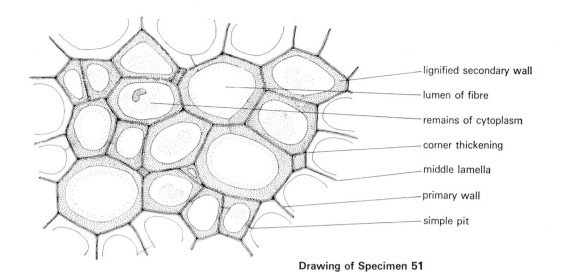

lignified secondary **wall**

lumen of fibre

remains of cytoplasm

corner thickening

middle lamella

primary wall

simple pit

Drawing of Specimen 51

lumen of fibre

overlapping tapered end walls

remains of cytoplasm

middle lamella

primary wall

lignified secondary wall

nucleus

Drawing of Specimen 52

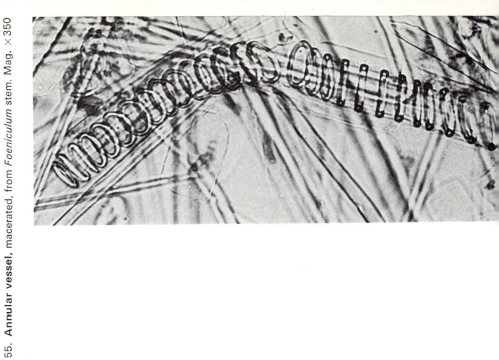

55. **Annular vessel**, macerated, from *Foeniculum* stem. Mag. ×350

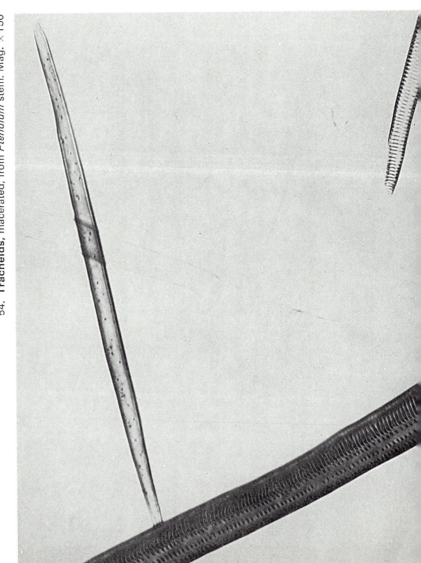

54. **Tracheids**, macerated, from *Pteridium* stem. Mag. ×150

53. **Sclereid**, macerated, from *Pyrus* fruit. Mag. ×400

branched or ramiform pit

lumen of brachysclereid (stone cell)

primary wall

secondary wall

simple pit

Drawing of Specimen 53

simple perforation plate

bend is artefact
caused in preparation of macerate

primary wall

Drawing of Specimen 55

secondary wall of annular rings

tapering closed end of tracheid

primary wall

secondary wall with scalariform thickening

Drawing of Specimen 54

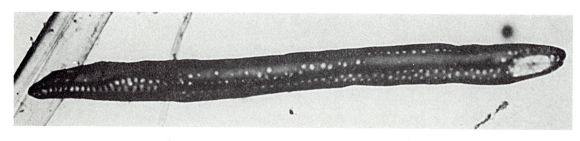

58. **Pitted vessel**, macerated, from *Foeniculum* stem. Mag. ×350

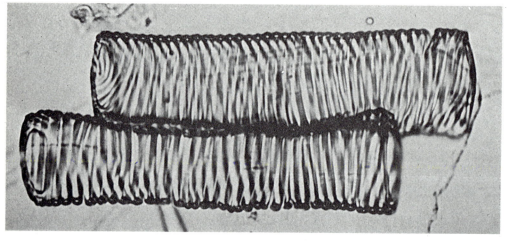

57. **Reticular vessel**, macerated, from *Foeniculum* stem. Mag. ×350

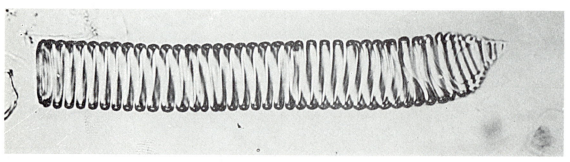

56. **Spiral vessel**, macerated, from *Foeniculum* stem. Mag. ×350

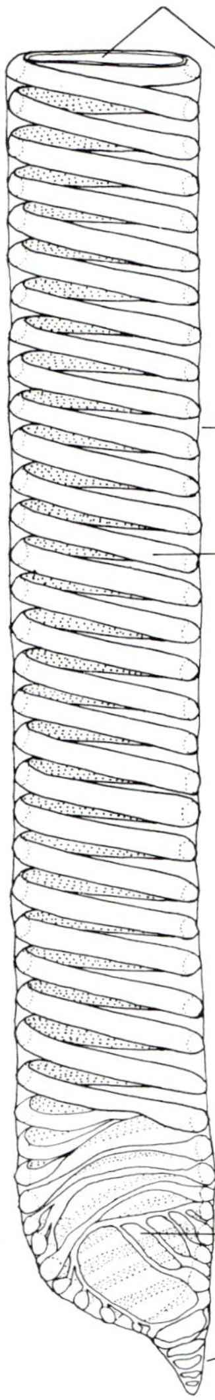

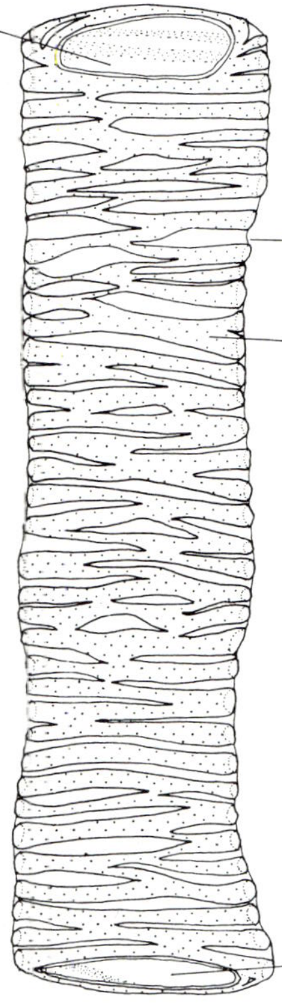

primary wall

secondary reticulate wall

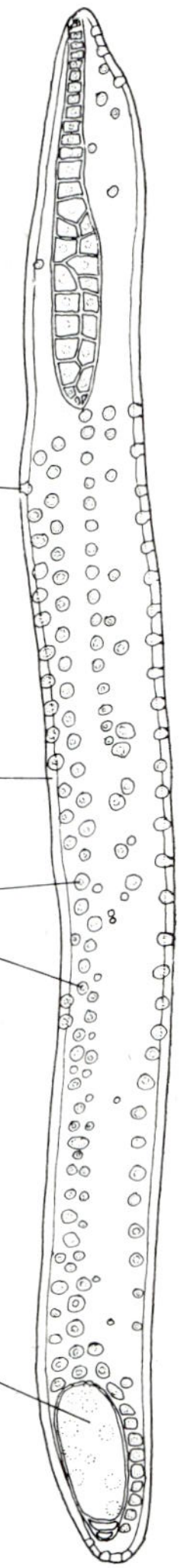

secondary wall

bordered pits

simple perforation plate

Drawing of Specimen 58

Drawing of Specimen 57

simple perforation plate

primary wall

spiral thickening
of secondary wall

scalariform perforation plate

tail

Drawing of Specimen 56

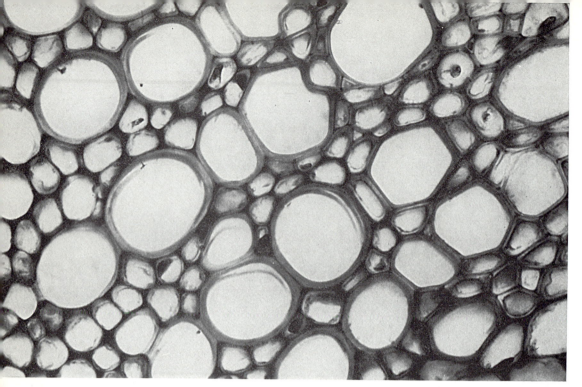

59. **Xylem,** TS, from *Helianthus* stem. Mag. ×600

60. **Xylem,** LS, from *Helianthus* stem. Mag. ×550

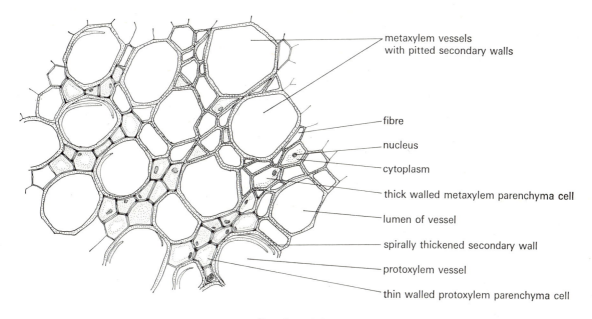

metaxylem vessels
with pitted secondary walls

fibre

nucleus

cytoplasm

thick walled metaxylem parenchyma cell

lumen of vessel

spirally thickened secondary wall

protoxylem vessel

thin walled protoxylem parenchyma cell

Drawing of Specimen 59

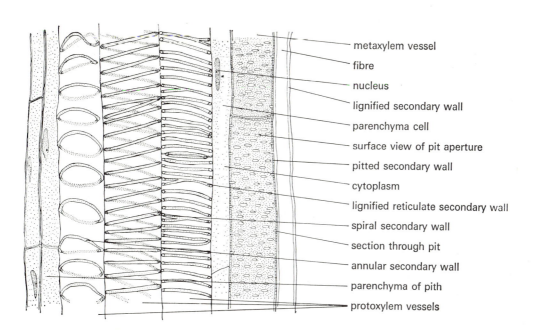

metaxylem vessel

fibre

nucleus

lignified secondary wall

parenchyma cell

surface view of pit aperture

pitted secondary wall

cytoplasm

lignified reticulate secondary wall

spiral secondary wall

section through pit

annular secondary wall

parenchyma of pith

protoxylem vessels

Drawing of Specimen 60

61. **Phloem,** TS, from *Helianthus* stem. Mag. ×450

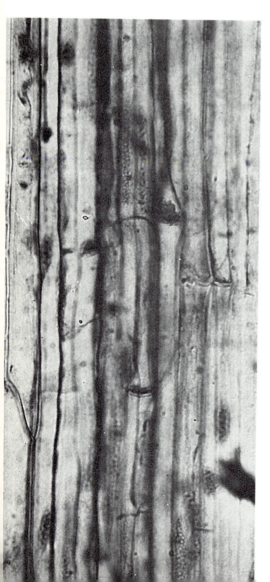

62. **Phloem,** LS, from *Helianthus* stem. Mag. ×450

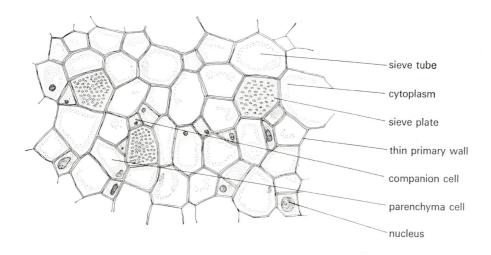

— sieve tube

— cytoplasm

— sieve plate

— thin primary wall

— companion cell

— parenchyma cell

— nucleus

Drawing of Specimen 61

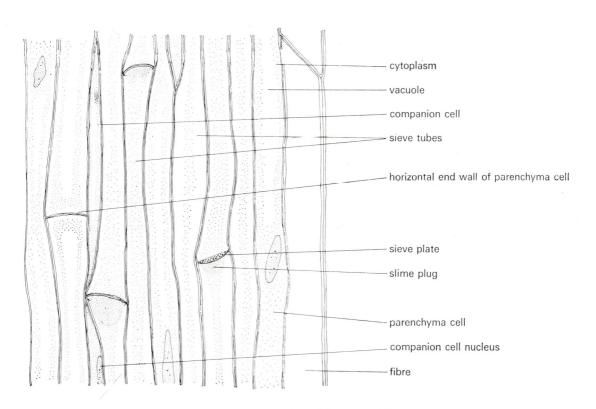

— cytoplasm

— vacuole

— companion cell

— sieve tubes

— horizontal end wall of parenchyma cell

— sieve plate

— slime plug

— parenchyma cell

— companion cell nucleus

— fibre

Drawing of Specimen 62

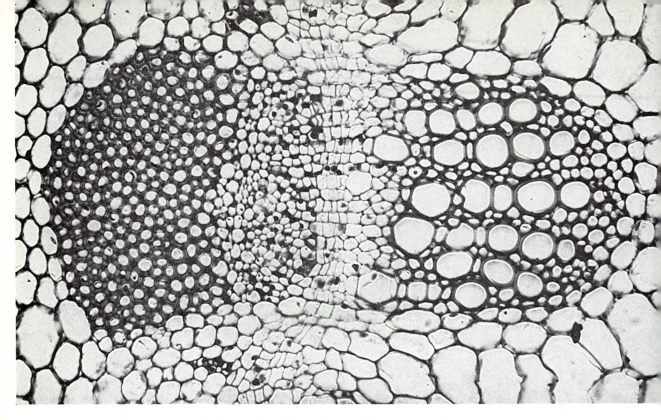

65. **Vascular bundle,** TS, from *Helianthus* stem. Mag. ×150

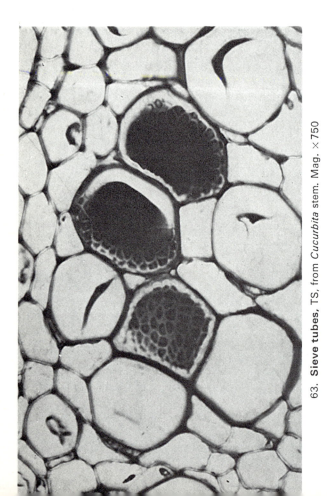

63. **Sieve tubes,** TS, from *Cucurbita* stem. Mag. ×750

64. **Sieve tubes,** LS, from *Cucurbita* stem. Mag. ×450

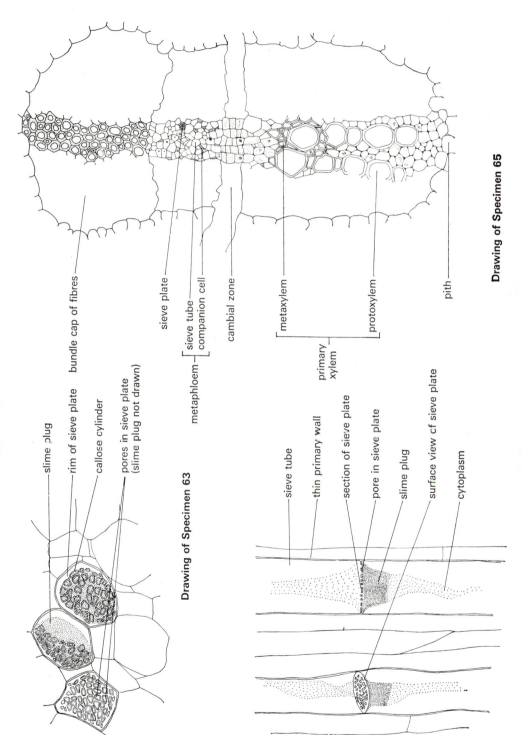

slime plug

rim of sieve plate

bundle cap of fibres

callose cylinder

pores in sieve plate
(slime plug not drawn)

sieve plate

metaphloem $\left[\begin{array}{l}\text{sieve tube}\\\text{companion cell}\end{array}\right.$

cambial zone

metaxylem

protoxylem

primary xylem

pith

Drawing of Specimen 63

Drawing of Specimen 65

sieve tube

thin primary wall

section of sieve plate

pore in sieve plate

slime plug

surface view cf sieve plate

cytoplasm

Drawing of Specimen 64

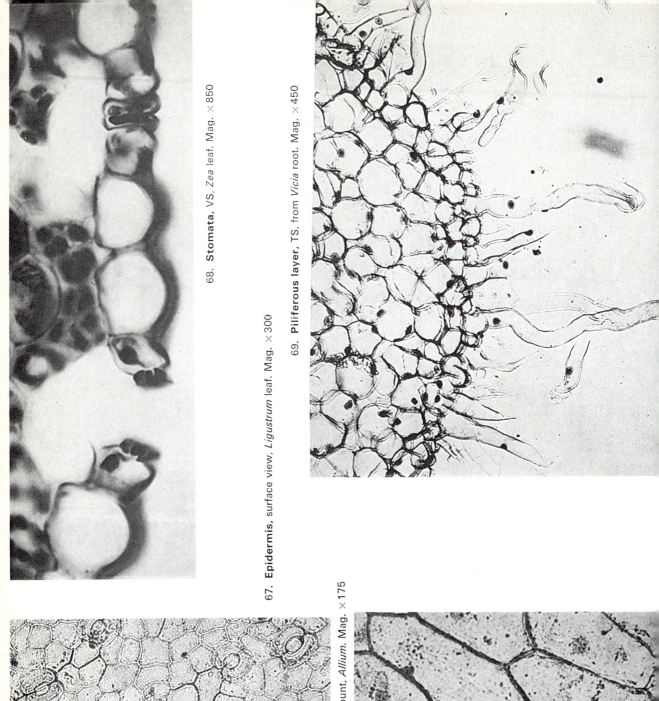

68. **Stomata**, VS, *Zea* leaf. Mag. ×850

69. **Piliferous layer**, TS, from *Vicia* root. Mag. ×450

67. **Epidermis**, surface view, *Ligustrum* leaf. Mag. ×300

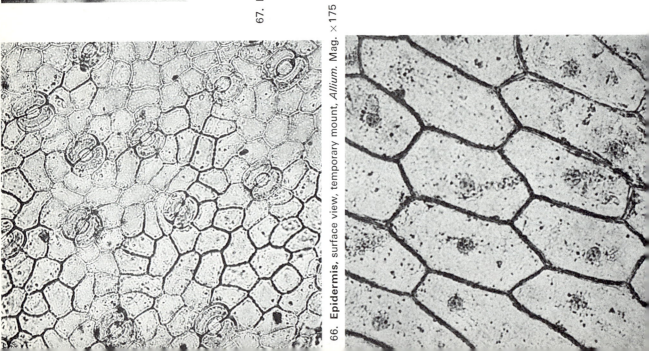

66. **Epidermis**, surface view, temporary mount, *Allium*. Mag. ×175

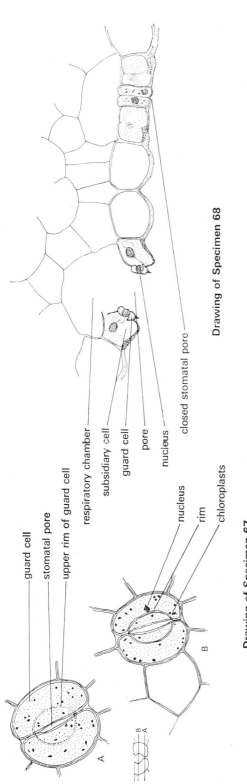

guard cell
stomatal pore
upper rim of guard cell
respiratory chamber
subsidiary cell
guard cell
pore
nucleus
closed stomatal pore

nucleus
rim
chloroplasts

Drawing of Specimen 68

Drawing of Specimen 67

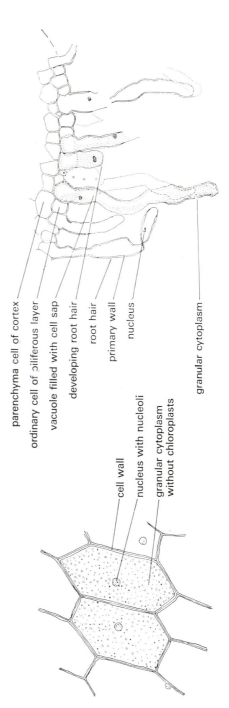

parenchyma cell of cortex
ordinary cell of piliferous layer
vacuole filled with cell sap
developing root hair
root hair
primary wall
nucleus
granular cytoplasm

cell wall
nucleus with nucleoli
granular cytoplasm
without chloroplasts

Drawing of Specimen 69

Drawing of Specimen 66

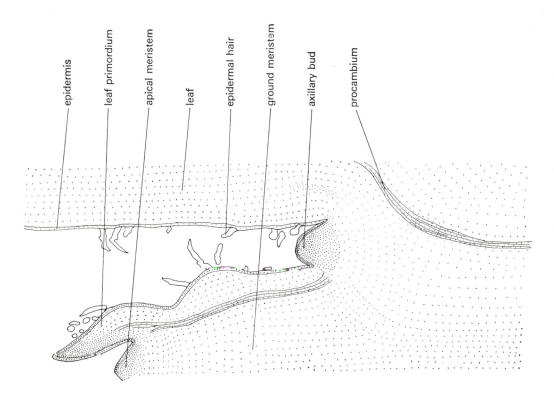

epidermis

leaf primordium

apical meristem

leaf

epidermal hair

ground meristem

axillary bud

procambium

Drawing of Specimen 70

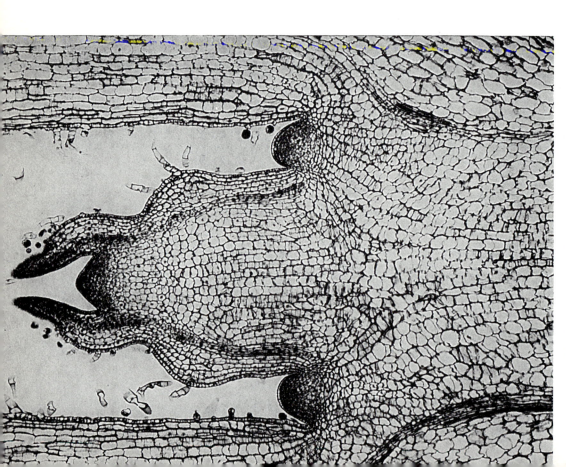

70. **Stem apex, LS,** *Coleus.* Mag. ×85

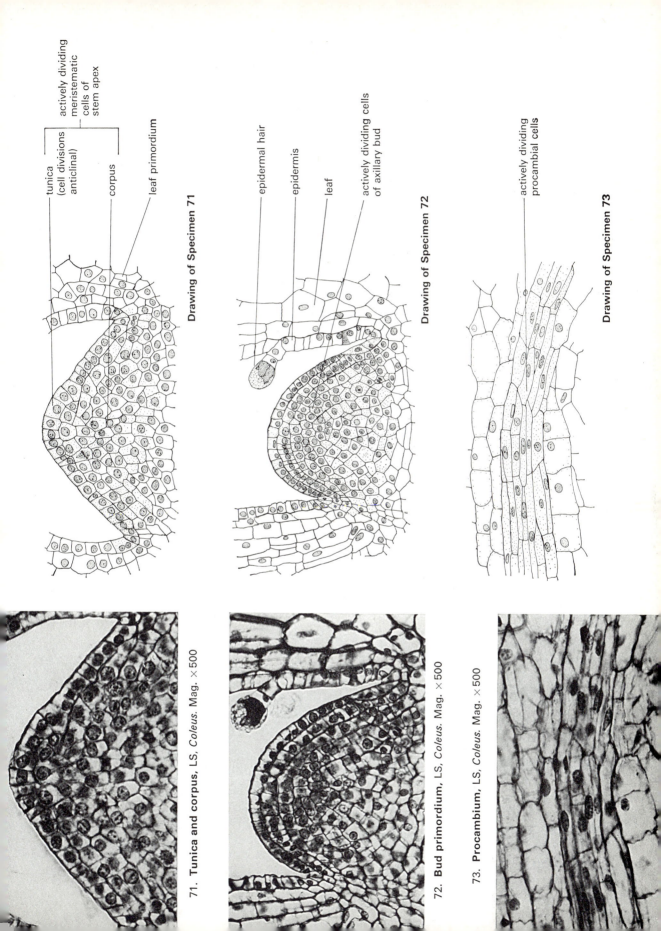

actively dividing meristematic cells of stem apex

tunica (cell divisions anticlinal)

corpus

leaf primordium

Drawing of Specimen 71

71. **Tunica and corpus, LS, *Coleus*. Mag. × 500**

epidermal hair

epidermis

leaf

actively dividing cells of axillary bud

Drawing of Specimen 72

72. **Bud primordium, LS, *Coleus*. Mag. × 500**

actively dividing procambial cells

Drawing of Specimen 73

73. **Procambium, LS, *Coleus*. Mag. × 500**

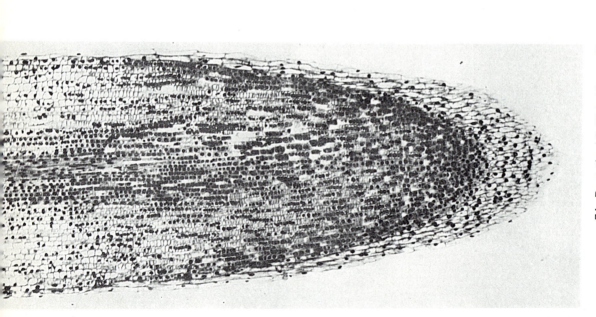

75. **Mitosis stages,** from LS *Vicia* root tip (74). Mag. × 400

74. **Root tip,** LS, *Vicia.* Mag. × 50

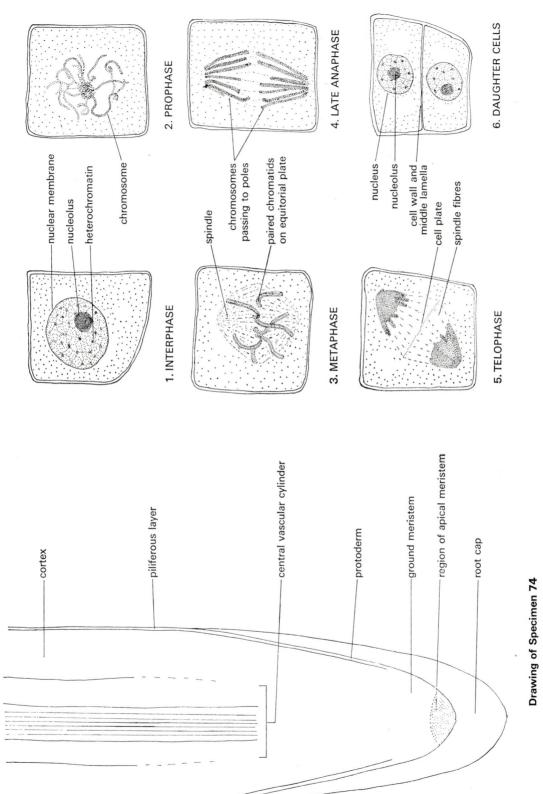

nuclear membrane
nucleolus
heterochromatin
chromosome

1. INTERPHASE

2. PROPHASE

spindle
chromosomes passing to poles
paired chromatids on equitorial plate

3. METAPHASE

4. LATE ANAPHASE

nucleus
nucleolus
cell wall and middle lamella
cell plate
spindle fibres

5. TELOPHASE

6. DAUGHTER CELLS

Drawings from Specimen 75 showing stages in mitosis

cortex

piliferous layer

central vascular cylinder

protoderm

ground meristem

region of apical meristem

root cap

Drawing of Specimen 74

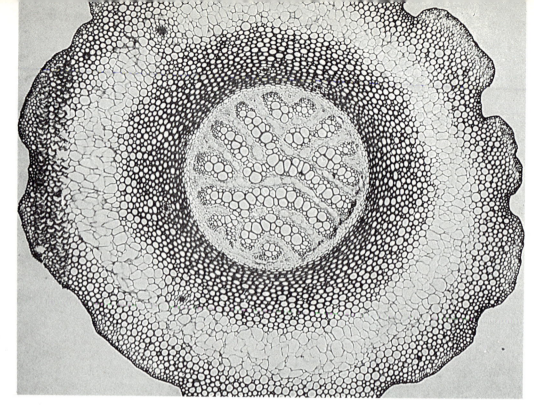

76. **Stem**, TS, *Lycopodium* sp. Mag. ×60

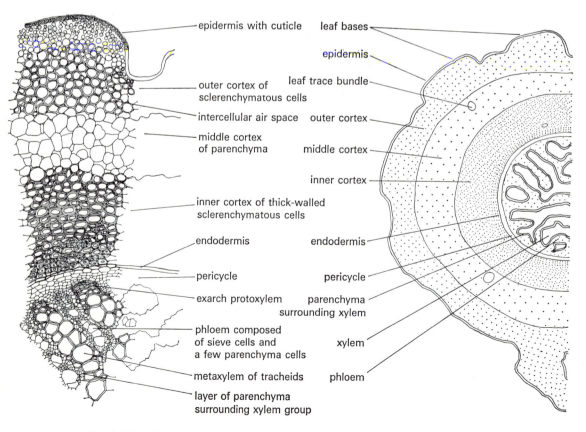

epidermis with cuticle

outer cortex of
sclerenchymatous cells

intercellular air space

middle cortex
of parenchyma

inner cortex of thick-walled
sclerenchymatous cells

endodermis

pericycle

exarch protoxylem

phloem composed
of sieve cells and
a few parenchyma cells

metaxylem of tracheids

layer of parenchyma
surrounding xylem group

leaf bases

epidermis

leaf trace bundle

outer cortex

middle cortex

inner cortex

endodermis

pericycle

parenchyma
surrounding xylem

xylem

phloem

Detail of Specimen 76

Drawing of Specimen 76

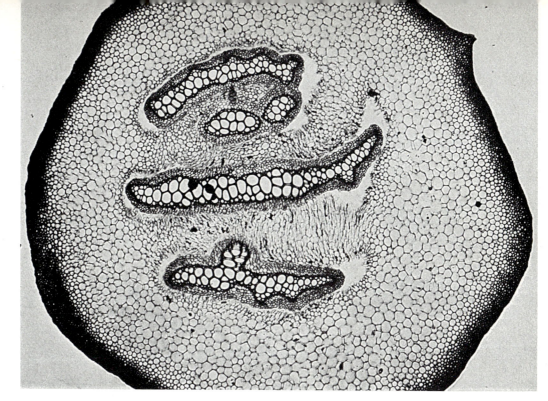

77. **Stem,** TS, *Selaginella* sp. Mag. ×45

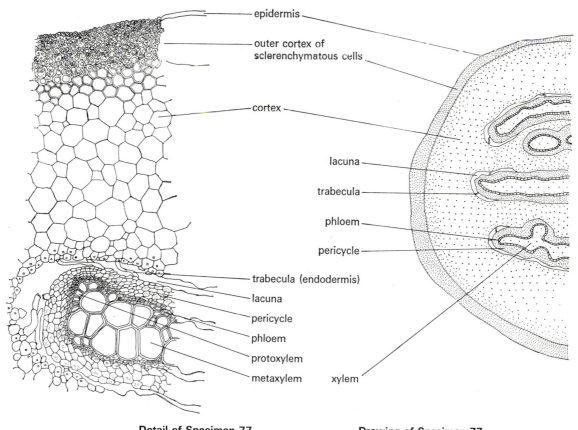

epidermis

outer cortex of
sclerenchymatous cells

cortex

lacuna

trabecula

phloem

pericycle

trabecula (endodermis)

lacuna

pericycle

phloem

protoxylem

metaxylem

xylem

Detail of Specimen 77   **Drawing of Specimen 77**

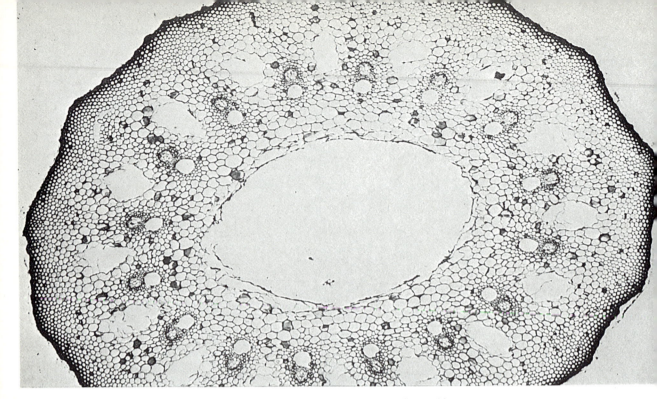

78. **Rhizome,** TS, *Equisetum* sp. Mag. ×60

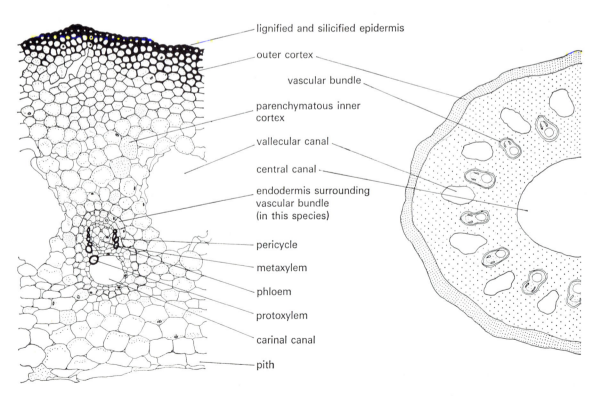

lignified and silicified epidermis

outer cortex

vascular bundle

parenchymatous inner cortex

vallecular canal

central canal

endodermis surrounding vascular bundle (in this species)

pericycle

metaxylem

phloem

protoxylem

carinal canal

pith

Detail of Specimen 78   **Drawing of Specimen 78**

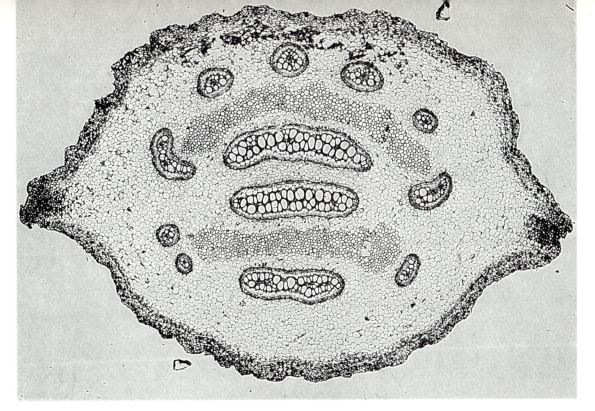

79. Rhizome, TS, *Pteridium.* Mag. ×25

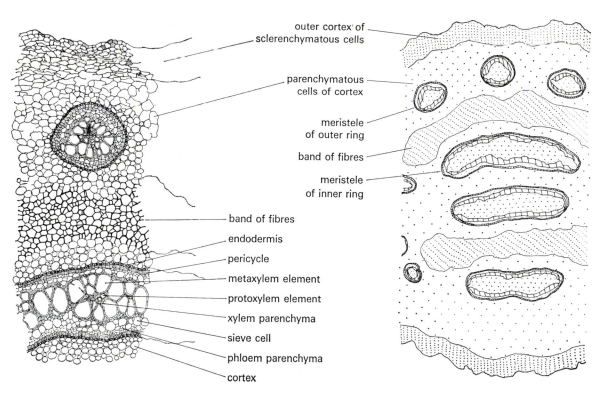

outer cortex of
sclerenchymatous cells

parenchymatous
cells of cortex

meristele
of outer ring

band of fibres

meristele
of inner ring

band of fibres

endodermis

pericycle

metaxylem element

protoxylem element

xylem parenchyma

sieve cell

phloem parenchyma

cortex

Detail of Specimen 79

Drawing of Specimen 79

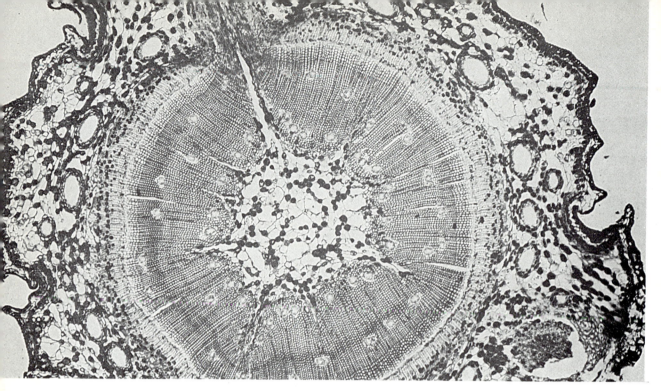

80. *Pinus*, young stem, TS. Mag. ×25

81. *Pinus*, young stem, RLS. Mag. ×25

82. *Pinus*, young stem, TLS. Mag. ×25

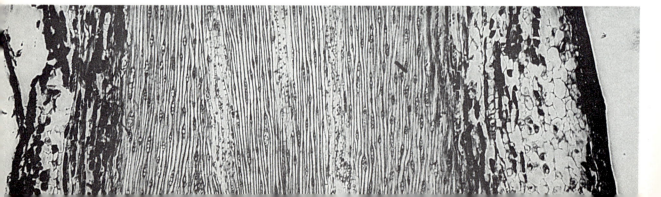

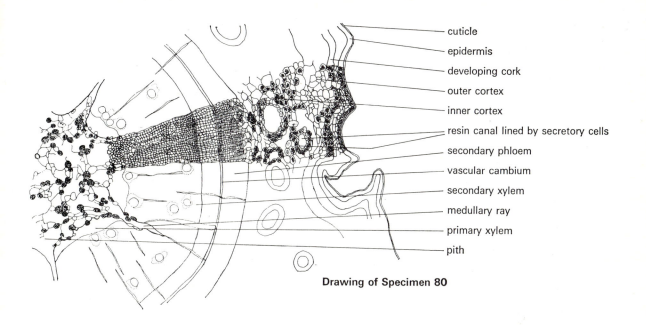

cuticle
epidermis
developing cork
outer cortex
inner cortex
resin canal lined by secretory cells
secondary phloem
vascular cambium
secondary xylem
medullary ray
primary xylem
pith

Drawing of Specimen 80

Drawing of Specimen 81

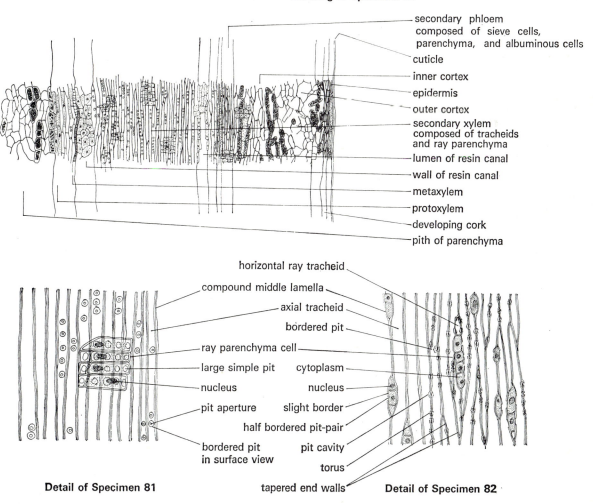

secondary phloem
composed of sieve cells,
parenchyma, and albuminous cells
cuticle
inner cortex
epidermis
outer cortex
secondary xylem
composed of tracheids
and ray parenchyma
lumen of resin canal
wall of resin canal
metaxylem
protoxylem
developing cork
pith of parenchyma

horizontal ray tracheid
compound middle lamella
axial tracheid
bordered pit
ray parenchyma cell
large simple pit   cytoplasm
nucleus   nucleus
pit aperture   slight border
half bordered pit-pair
bordered pit   pit cavity
in surface view
torus
tapered end walls

Detail of Specimen 81   **Detail of Specimen 82**

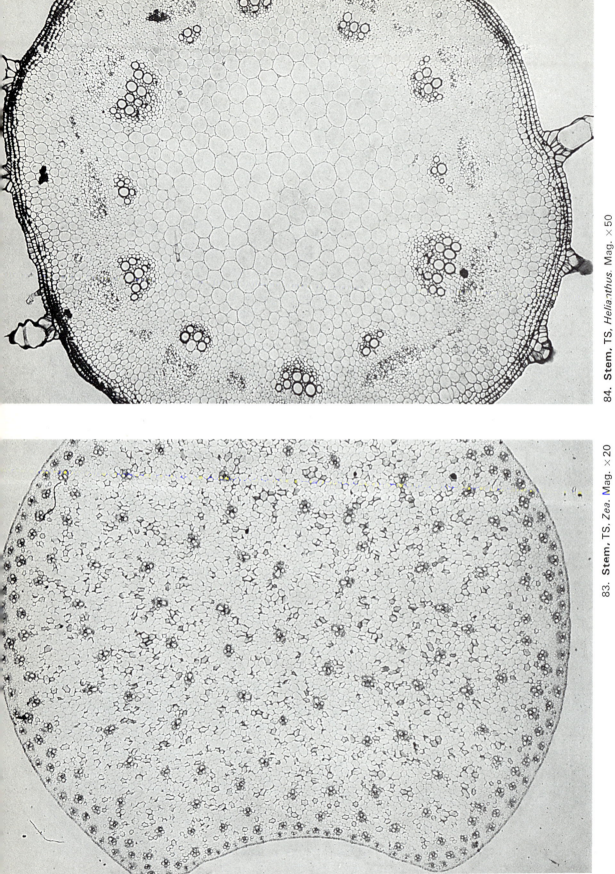

84. **Stem**, TS, *Helianthus*. Mag. ×50

83. **Stem**, TS, *Zea*. Mag. ×20

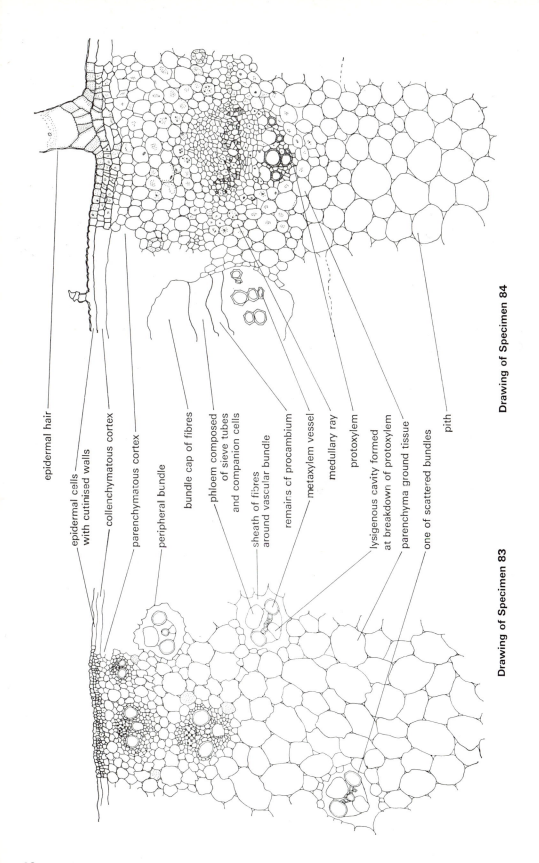

epidermal hair

epidermal cells
with cutinised walls

collenchymatous cortex

parenchymatous cortex

peripheral bundle

bundle cap of fibres

phloem composed
of sieve tubes
and companion cells

sheath of fibres
around vascular bundle

remains of procambium

metaxylem vessel

medullary ray

protoxylem

lysigenous cavity formed
at breakdown of protoxylem

parenchyma ground tissue

one of scattered bundles

pith

Drawing of Specimen 84

Drawing of Specimen 83

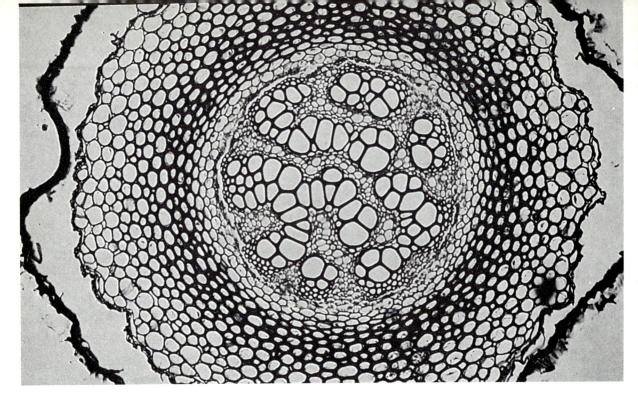

85. **Root**, TS, *Lycopodium*. Mag. ×80

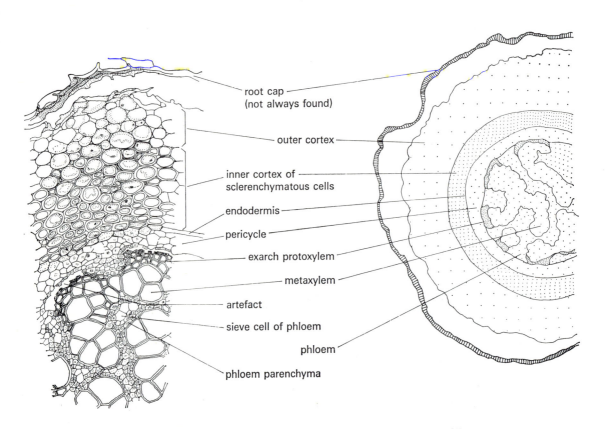

root cap
(not always found)

outer cortex

inner cortex of
sclerenchymatous cells

endodermis

pericycle

exarch protoxylem

metaxylem

artefact

sieve cell of phloem

phloem

phloem parenchyma

Detail of Specimen 85   **Drawing of Specimen 85**

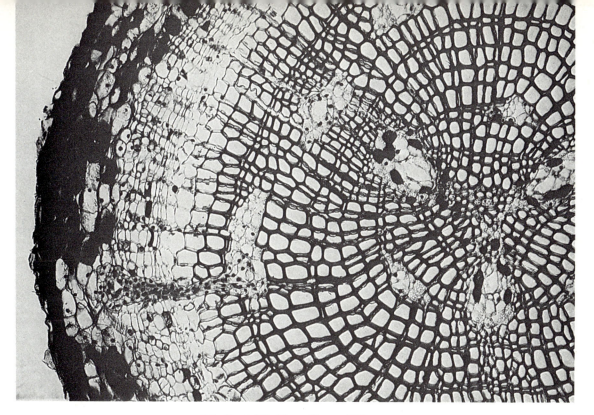

86. **Root,** TS, *Pinus,* Mag. ×100

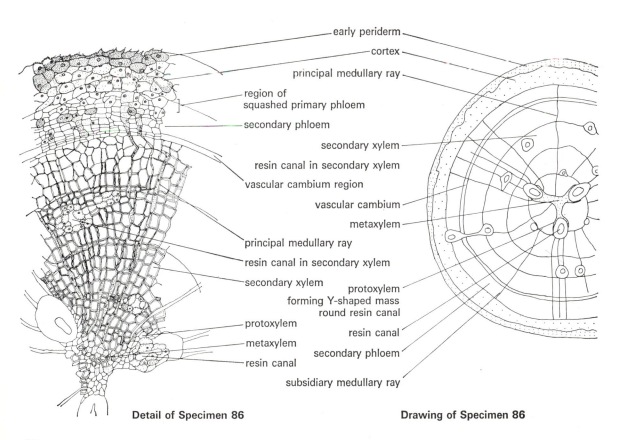

early periderm

cortex

principal medullary ray

region of
squashed primary phloem

secondary phloem

secondary xylem

resin canal in secondary xylem

vascular cambium region

vascular cambium

metaxylem

principal medullary ray

resin canal in secondary xylem

secondary xylem

protoxylem
forming Y-shaped mass
round resin canal

protoxylem

metaxylem

resin canal

resin canal

secondary phloem

subsidiary medullary ray

Detail of Specimen 86

Drawing of Specimen 86

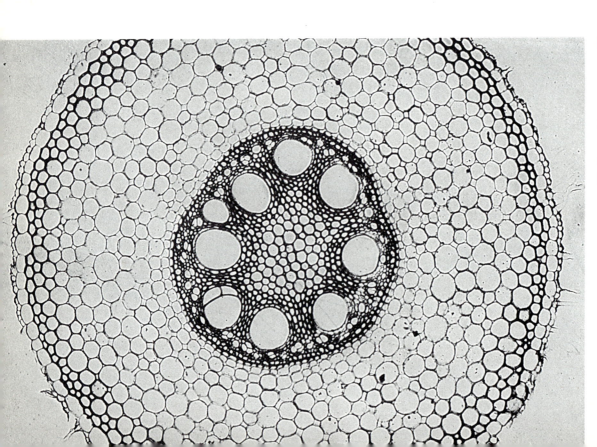

88. **Root,** TS, *Ranunculus.* Mag. ×125

87. **Root,** TS, *Zea.* Mag. ×50

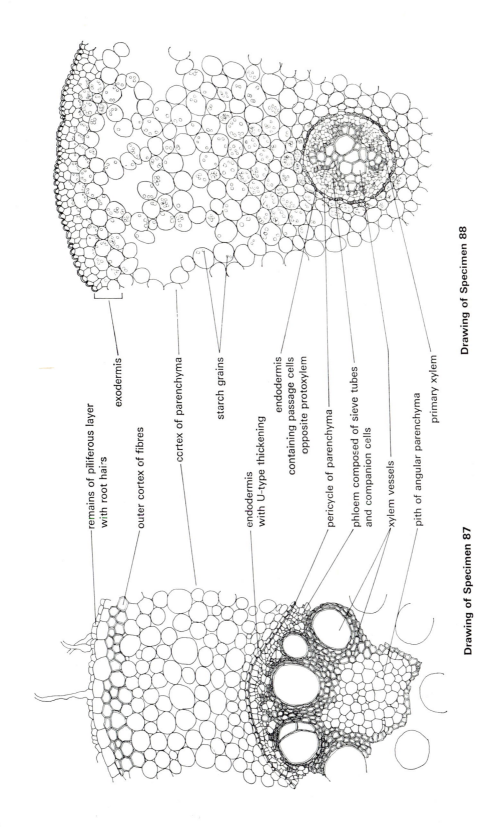

Drawing of Specimen 88

remains of piliferous layer
with root hairs

exodermis

outer cortex of fibres

cortex of parenchyma

starch grains

endodermis
with U-type thickening

endodermis
containing passage cells
opposite protoxylem

pericycle of parenchyma

phloem composed of sieve tubes
and companion cells

xylem vessels

pith of angular parenchyma

primary xylem

Drawing of Specimen 87

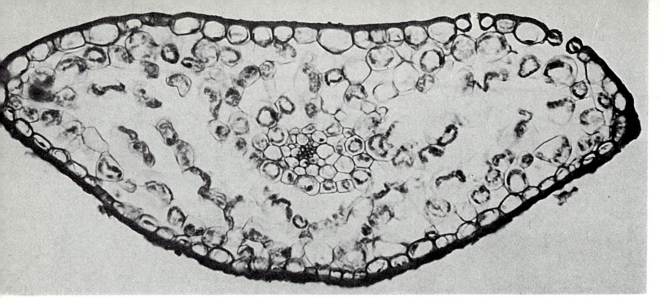

89. **Leaf**, TS, *Lycopodium*. Mag. ×100

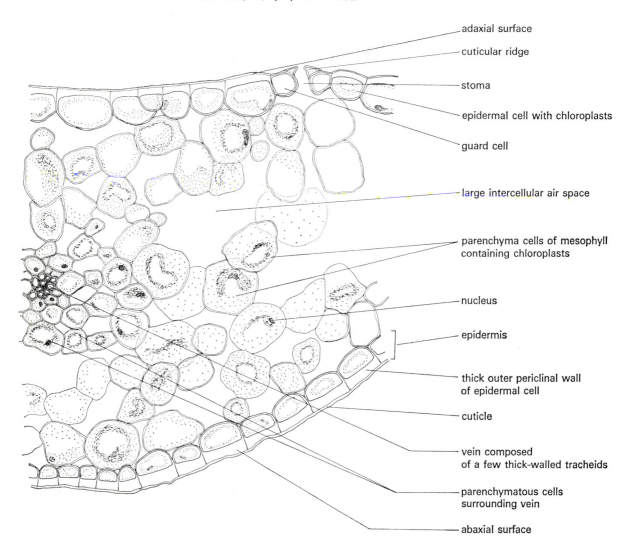

adaxial surface

cuticular ridge

stoma

epidermal cell with chloroplasts

guard cell

large intercellular air space

parenchyma cells of **mesophyll** containing chloroplasts

nucleus

epidermis

thick outer periclinal wall of epidermal cell

cuticle

vein composed of a few thick-walled tracheids

parenchymatous cells surrounding vein

abaxial surface

Drawing of Specimen 89

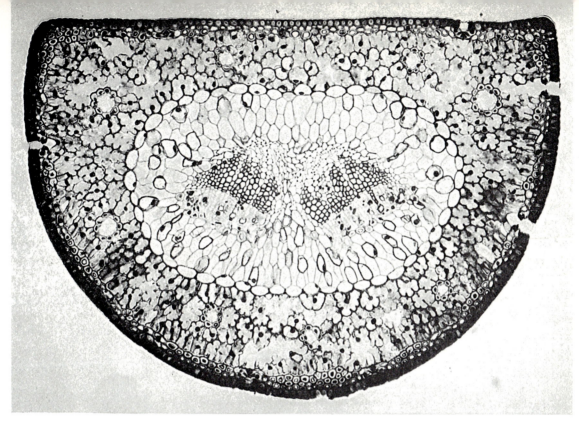

90. **Leaf,** TS, *Pinus.* Mag. ×120

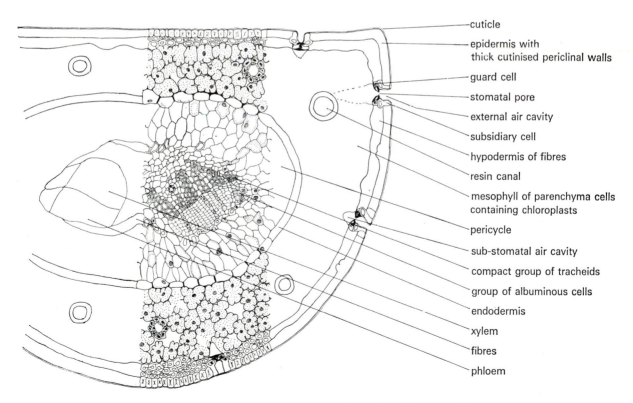

cuticle

epidermis with
thick cutinised periclinal walls

guard cell

stomatal pore

external air cavity

subsidiary cell

hypodermis of fibres

resin canal

mesophyll of parenchyma cells
containing chloroplasts

pericycle

sub-stomatal air cavity

compact group of tracheids

group of albuminous cells

endodermis

xylem

fibres

phloem

Drawing of Specimen 90

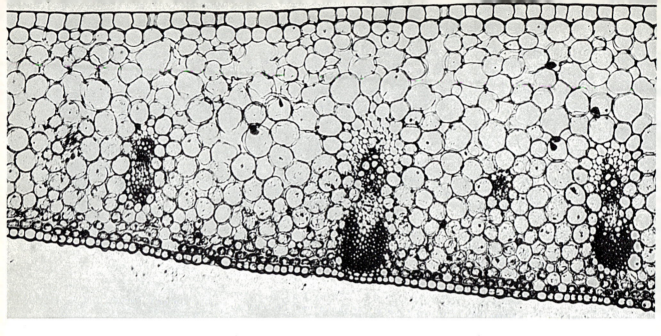

91. **Leaf**, TS, *Iris.* Mag. ×65

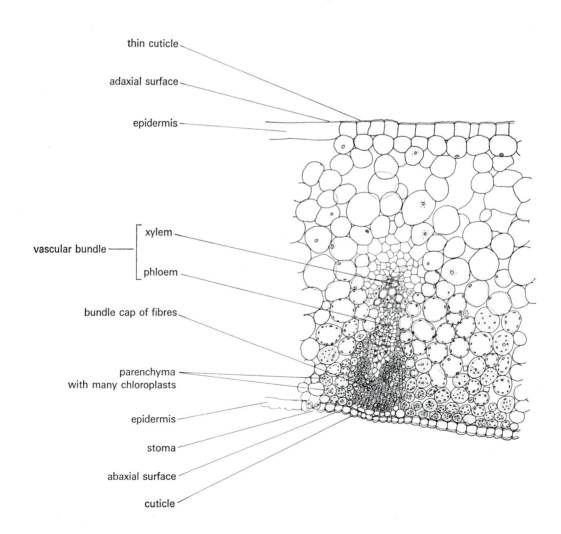

thin cuticle

adaxial surface

epidermis

vascular bundle — [xylem

phloem]

bundle cap of fibres

parenchyma
with many chloroplasts

epidermis

stoma

abaxial surface

cuticle

Drawing of Specimen 91

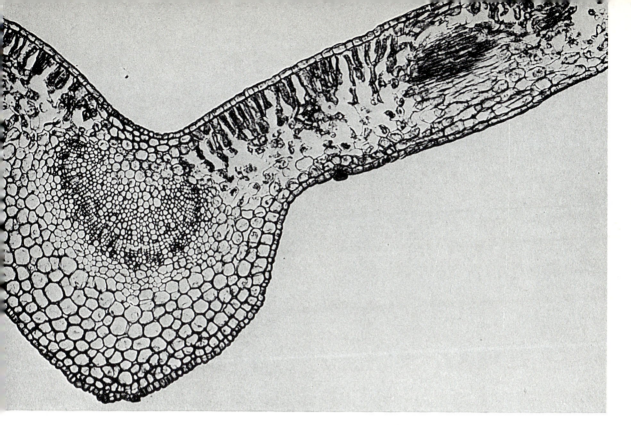

92. **Leaf**, TS, *Ligustrum*. Mag. ×100

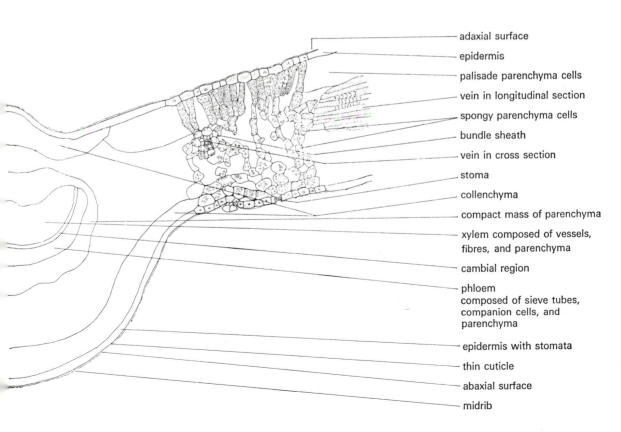

adaxial surface

epidermis

palisade parenchyma cells

vein in longitudinal section

spongy parenchyma cells

bundle sheath

vein in cross section

stoma

collenchyma

compact mass of parenchyma

xylem composed of vessels, fibres, and parenchyma

cambial region

phloem
composed of sieve tubes, companion cells, and parenchyma

epidermis with stomata

thin cuticle

abaxial surface

midrib

Drawing of Specimen 92

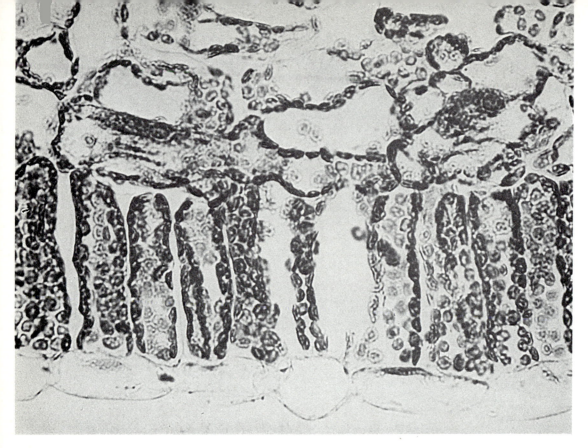

93. **Palisade layer,** VS, *Ligustrum.* Mag. ×320

94. **Palisade layer,** HS. *Ligustrum.* Mag. ×320

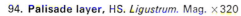

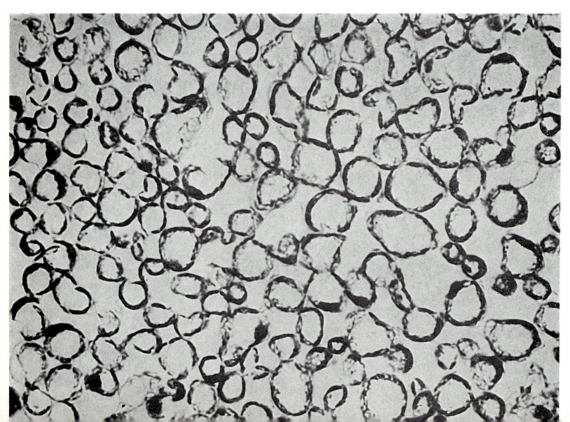

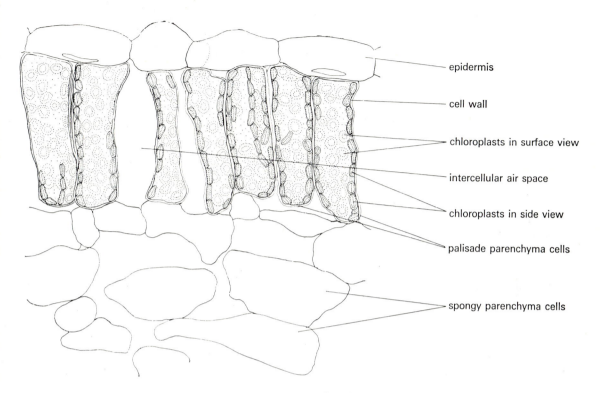

epidermis

cell wall

chloroplasts in surface view

intercellular air space

chloroplasts in side view

palisade parenchyma cells

spongy parenchyma cells

Drawing of Specimen 93

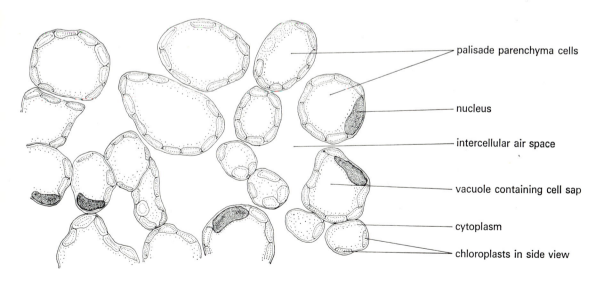

palisade parenchyma cells

nucleus

intercellular air space

vacuole containing cell sap

cytoplasm

chloroplasts in side view

Drawing of Specimen 94

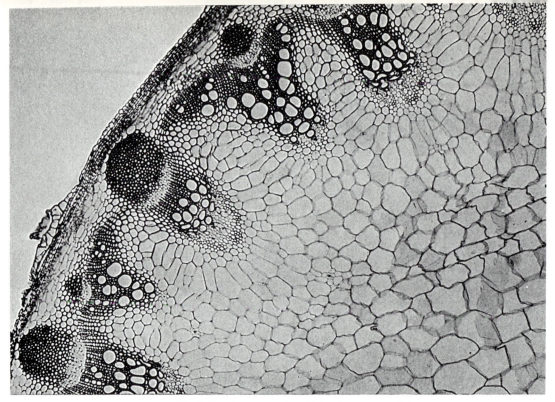

95. **Stem**, TS, *Helianthus,* secondary thickening. Mag. ×75

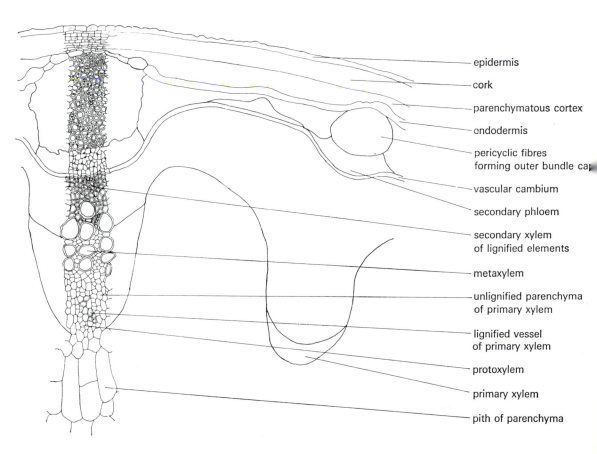

epidermis

cork

parenchymatous cortex

endodermis

pericyclic fibres
forming outer bundle cap

vascular cambium

secondary phloem

secondary xylem
of lignified elements

metaxylem

unlignified parenchyma
of primary xylem

lignified vessel
of primary xylem

protoxylem

primary xylem

pith of parenchyma

Drawing of Specimen 95

96. **Stem,** TS, *Pinus,* old. Mag. ×30

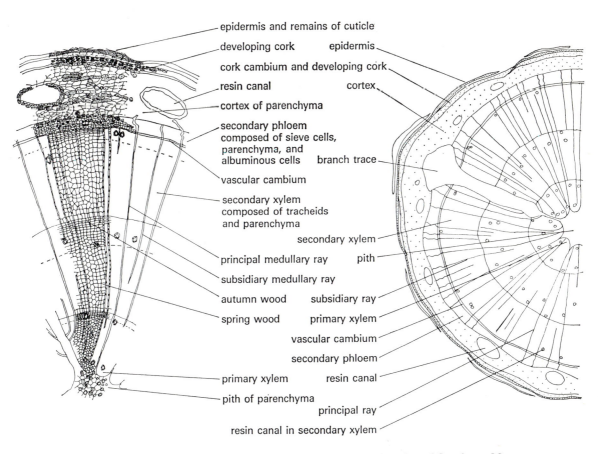

epidermis and remains of cuticle

developing cork   epidermis

cork cambium and developing cork

resin canal   cortex

cortex of parenchyma

secondary phloem
composed of sieve cells,
parenchyma, and
albuminous cells   branch trace

vascular cambium

secondary xylem
composed of tracheids
and parenchyma

secondary xylem

principal medullary ray   pith

subsidiary medullary ray

autumn wood   subsidiary ray

spring wood   primary xylem

vascular cambium

secondary phloem

primary xylem   resin canal

pith of parenchyma

principal ray

resin canal in secondary xylem

Detail of Specimen 96   **Drawing of Specimen 96**

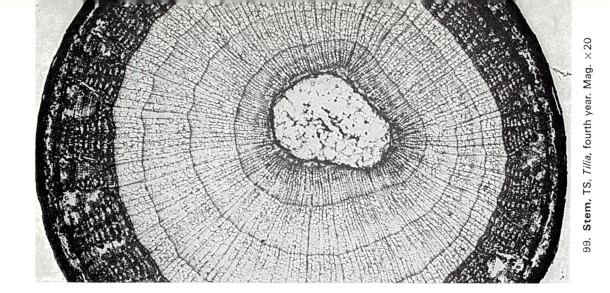

99. **Stem**, TS, *Tilia*, fourth year. Mag. ×20

98. **Stem**, TS, *Tilia*, second year. Mag. ×20

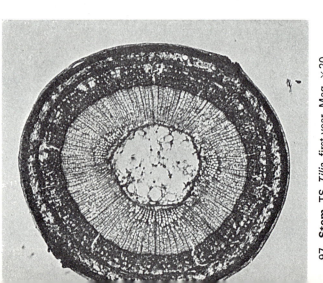

97. **Stem**, TS, *Tilia*, first year. Mag. ×20

remains of epidermis
cork
secondary phloem
secondary xylem
of first year's growth
collenchymatous cortex
primary xylem
cortex
pith
secondary phloem
wide phloem ray
band of sieve tubes
and companion cells
band of fibres
remains of epidermis
region of vascular cambium
cork
subsidiary
medullary ray
secondary phloem
principal
medullary ray
vascular cambium
secondary xylem
of second year's growth
secondary xylem
secondary xylem
of first year's growth
vessels
pith
fibres
autumn growth of first year
spring growth of first year
remains of epidermis
primary xylem
cork
pith
cork cambium

cortex

secondary phloem

vascular cambium

secondary xylem
of fourth year's growth
principal medullary ray
subsidiary medullary ray
secondary xylem
of first year's growth
primary xylem
pith

Drawing of part of Specimen 98

Drawings of portions of Specimens 97, 98, and 99

77

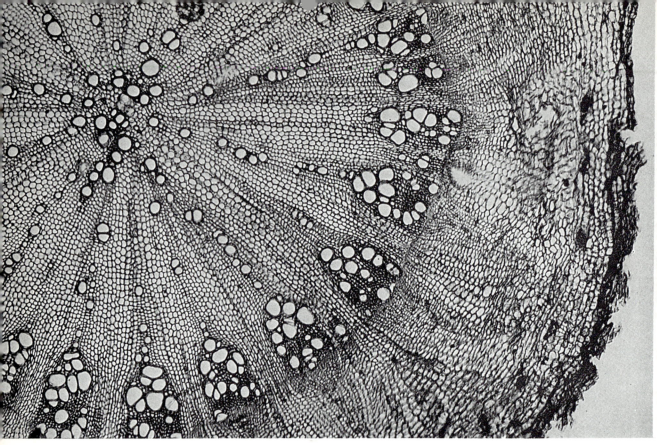

100. **Root,** TS, *Rumex,* secondary thickening. Mag. ×15

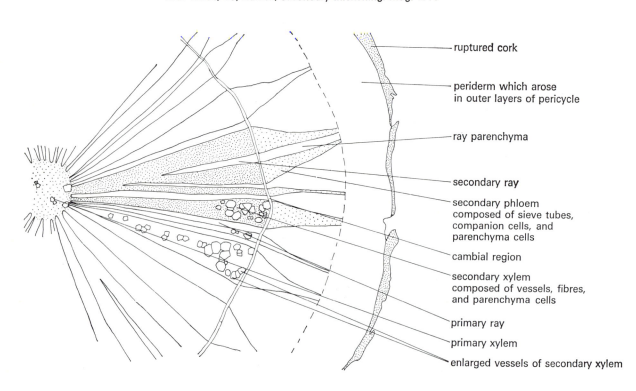

ruptured cork

periderm which arose
in outer layers of pericycle

ray parenchyma

secondary ray

secondary phloem
composed of sieve tubes,
companion cells, and
parenchyma cells

cambial region

secondary xylem
composed of vessels, fibres,
and parenchyma cells

primary ray

primary xylem

enlarged vessels of secondary xylem

Drawing of Specimen 100

101. Root, TS, epiphytic, *Dendrobium.* Mag. ×30

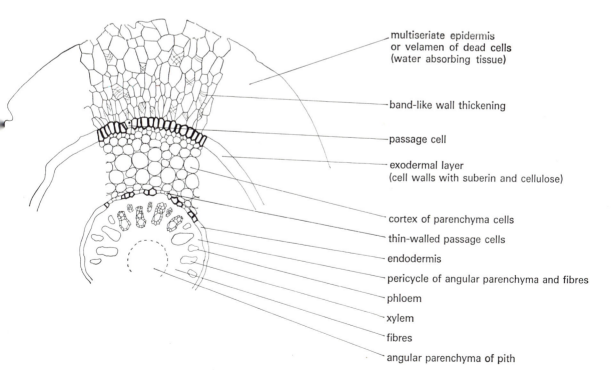

multiseriate epidermis
or velamen of dead cells
(water absorbing tissue)

band-like wall thickening

passage cell

exodermal layer
(cell walls with suberin and cellulose)

cortex of parenchyma cells

thin-walled passage cells

endodermis

pericycle of angular parenchyma and fibres

phloem

xylem

fibres

angular parenchyma of pith

Drawing of Specimen 101

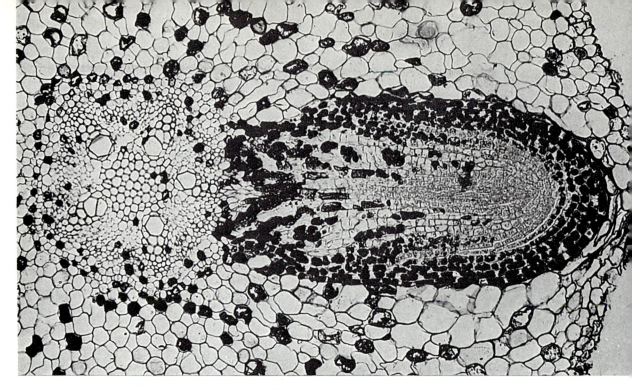

102. **Root**, TS, origin of lateral root, *Vicia*. Mag. ×100

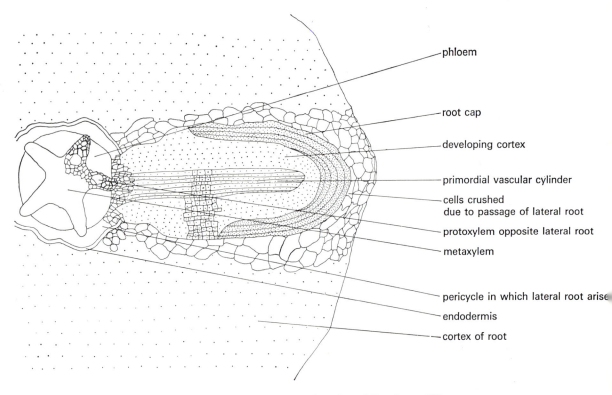

phloem

root cap

developing cortex

primordial vascular cylinder

cells crushed
due to passage of lateral root

protoxylem opposite lateral root

metaxylem

pericycle in which lateral root arise

endodermis

cortex of root

Drawing of Specimen 102

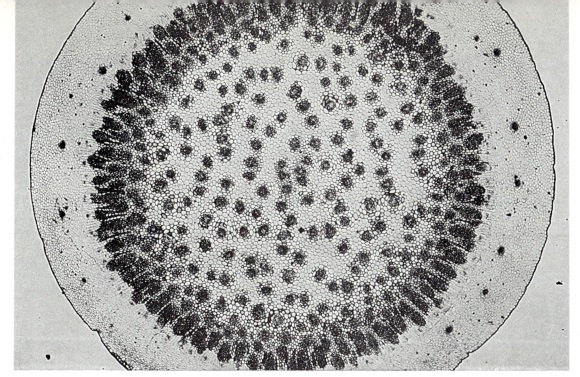

103. **Stem,** TS, *Dracaena.* Mag ×20

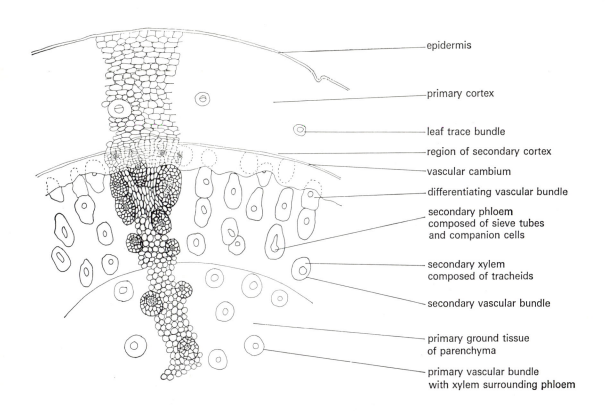

epidermis

primary cortex

leaf trace bundle

region of secondary cortex

vascular cambium

differentiating vascular bundle

secondary phloem
composed of sieve tubes
and companion cells

secondary xylem
composed of tracheids

secondary vascular bundle

primary ground tissue
of parenchyma

primary vascular bundle
with xylem surrounding phloem

Drawing of Specimen 103

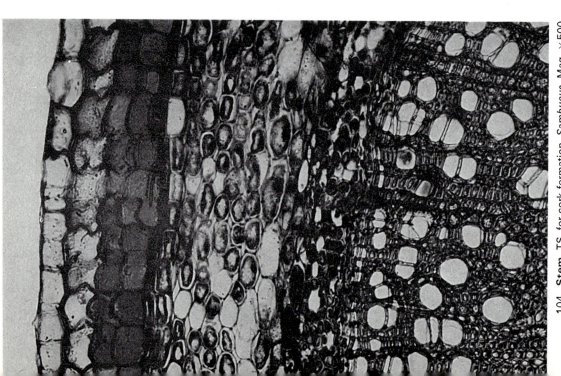

105. **Stem, TS, for cork formation,** *Ribes.* Mag. ×400

104. **Stem, TS, for cork formation,** *Sambucus.* Mag. ×500

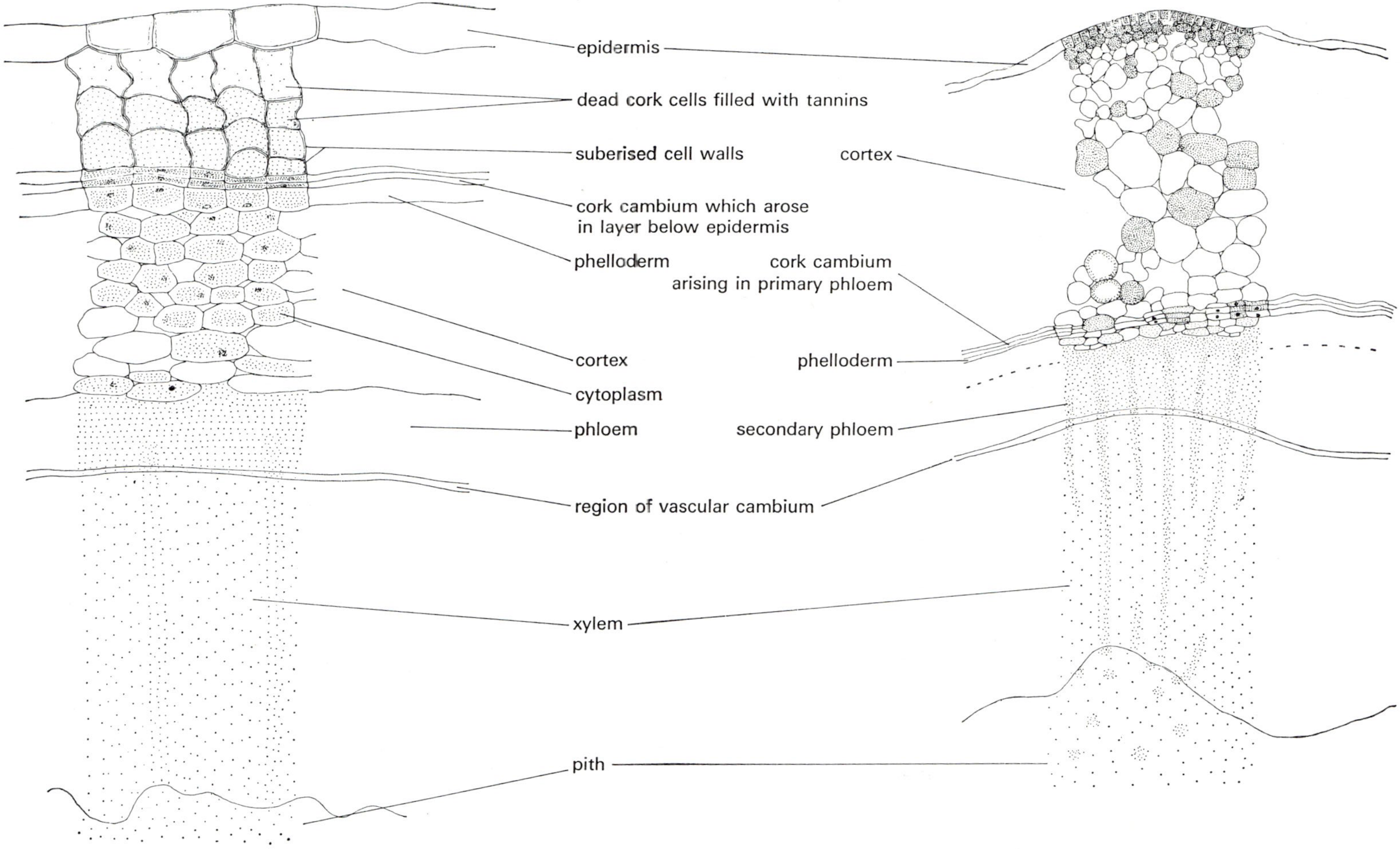

epidermis

dead cork cells filled with tannins

suberised cell walls

cortex

cork cambium which arose
in layer below epidermis

phelloderm

cork cambium
arising in primary phloem

phelloderm

cortex

cytoplasm

phloem

secondary phloem

region of vascular cambium

xylem

pith

Drawing of Specimen 105

Drawing of Specimen 104

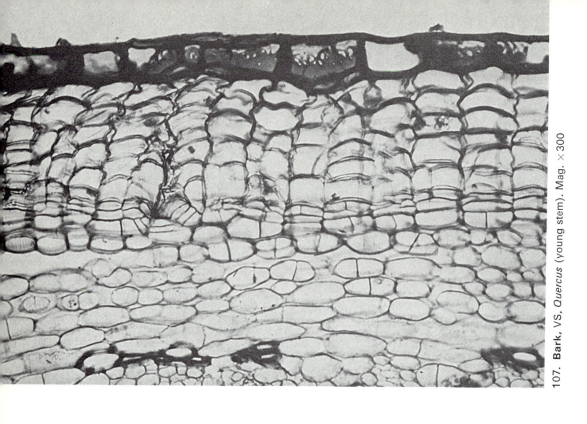

107. **Bark**, VS, *Quercus* (young stem). Mag. ×300

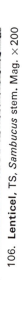

106. **Lenticel**, TS, *Sambucus* stem. Mag. ×200

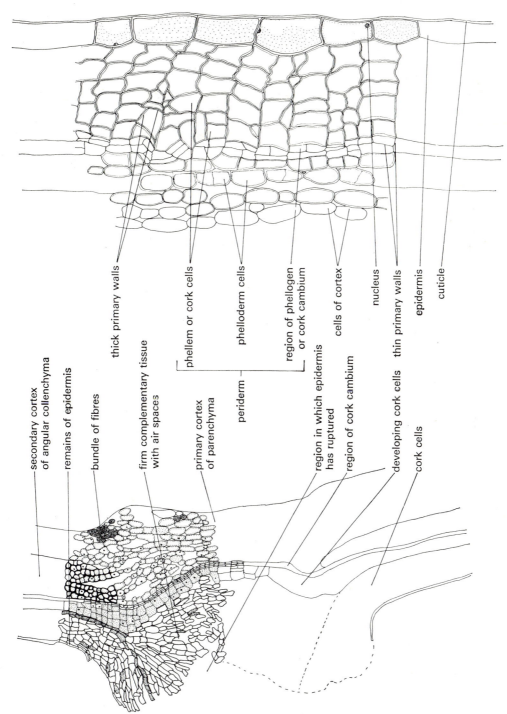

secondary cortex
of angular collenchyma

remains of epidermis

bundle of fibres

firm complementary tissue
with air spaces

primary cortex
of parenchyma

periderm

region in which epidermis
has ruptured

region of cork cambium

developing cork cells

cork cells

thick primary walls

phellem or cork cells

phelloderm cells

region of phellogen
or cork cambium

cells of cortex

nucleus

thin primary walls

epidermis

cuticle

Drawing of Specimen 107

Drawing of Specimen 106

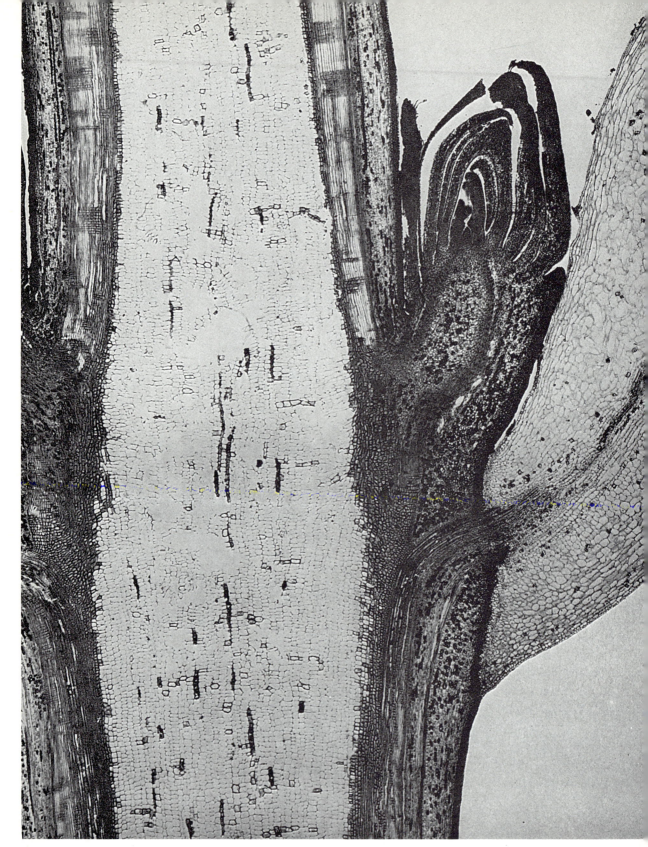

108. **Stem**, LS, for abscission, *Acer.* Mag. ×15

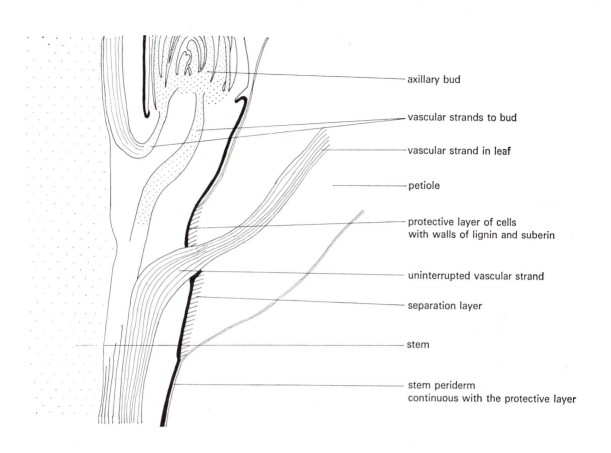

- axillary bud
- vascular strands to bud
- vascular strand in leaf
- petiole
- protective layer of cells with walls of lignin and suberin
- uninterrupted vascular strand
- separation layer
- stem
- stem periderm continuous with the protective layer

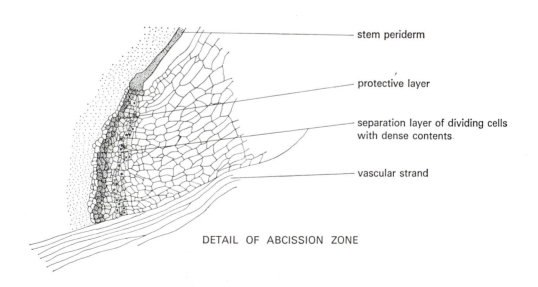

- stem periderm
- protective layer
- separation layer of dividing cells with dense contents.
- vascular strand

DETAIL OF ABCISSION ZONE

Drawing of Specimen 108

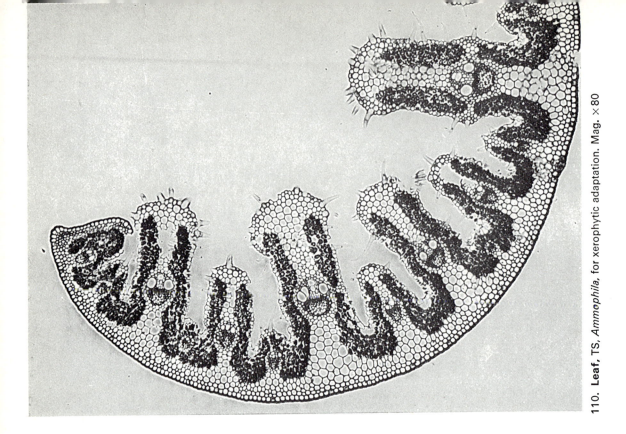

110. **Leaf**, TS, *Ammophila*, for xerophytic adaptation. Mag. ×80

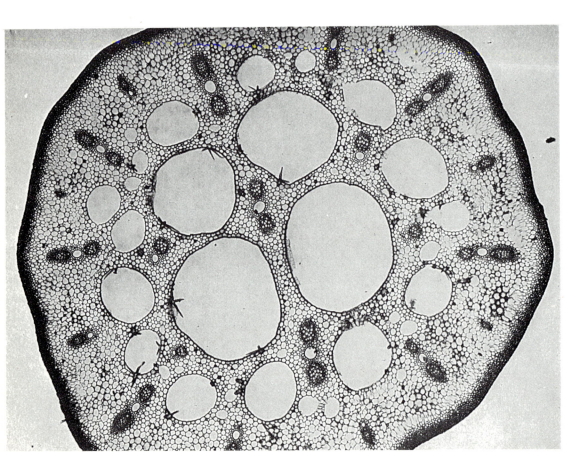

109. **Stem**, TS, *Nymphaea*, for hydrophytic adaptation. Mag. ×20

Drawing of Specimen 110

epidermis

endodermis

outer cortex
of compact parenchyma

inner cortex

phloem

vascular bundle

xylem

adaxial epidermis with
thin cuticle, stomata, and hairs

lacunae

group of bulliform or hinge cells

abaxial epidermis
with thick uneven cuticle

lysigenous xylem canal

bundle sheath
of compact parenchyma

phloem

asterosclereids
giving local support

photosynthetic
parenchyma cells of mesophyll

thin-walled fibres
of mesophyll

unicellular hair

Drawing of Specimen 109

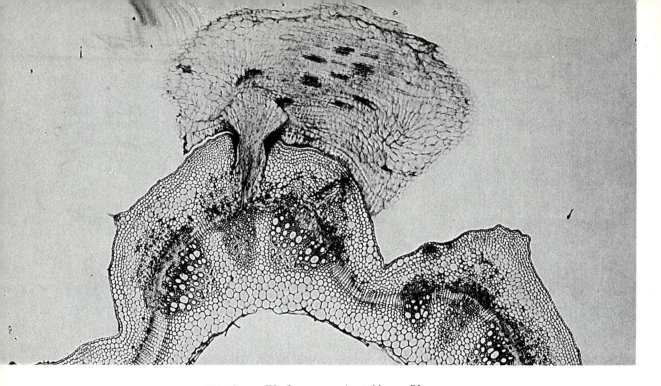

111. Stem, TS, *Cuscuta,* **on host. Mag. ×50**

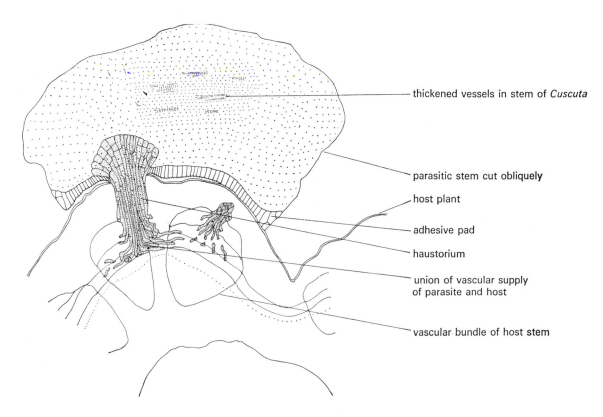

thickened vessels in stem of *Cuscuta*

parasitic stem cut obliquely

host plant

adhesive pad

haustorium

union of vascular supply of parasite and host

vascular bundle of host stem

Drawing of Specimen 111

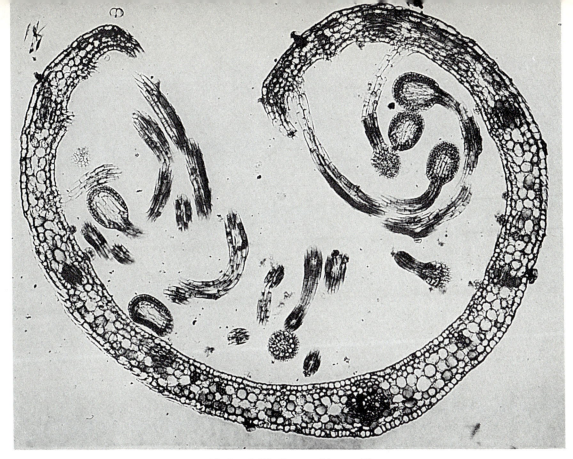

112. **Leaf,** TS, *Drosera.* Mag. ×45

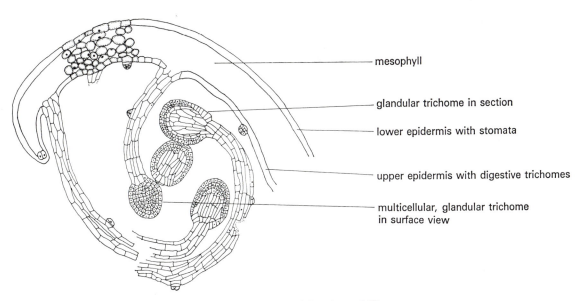

— mesophyll

— glandular trichome in section

— lower epidermis with stomata

— upper epidermis with digestive trichomes

— multicellular, glandular trichome in surface view

Drawing of Specimen 112

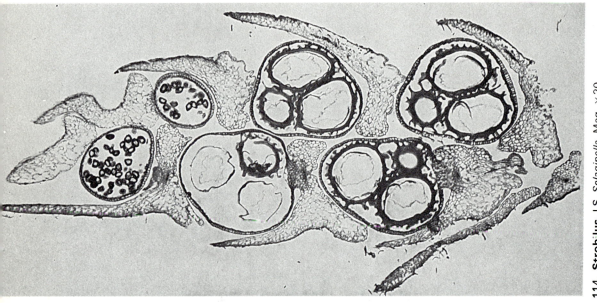

114. **Strobilus,** LS, *Selaginella.* Mag. × 20

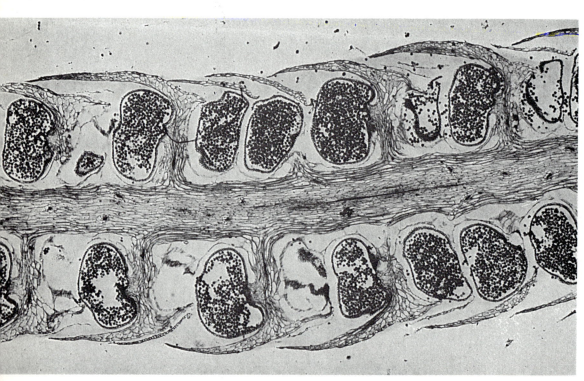

113. **Strobilus,** LS, *Lycopodium.* Mag. × 25

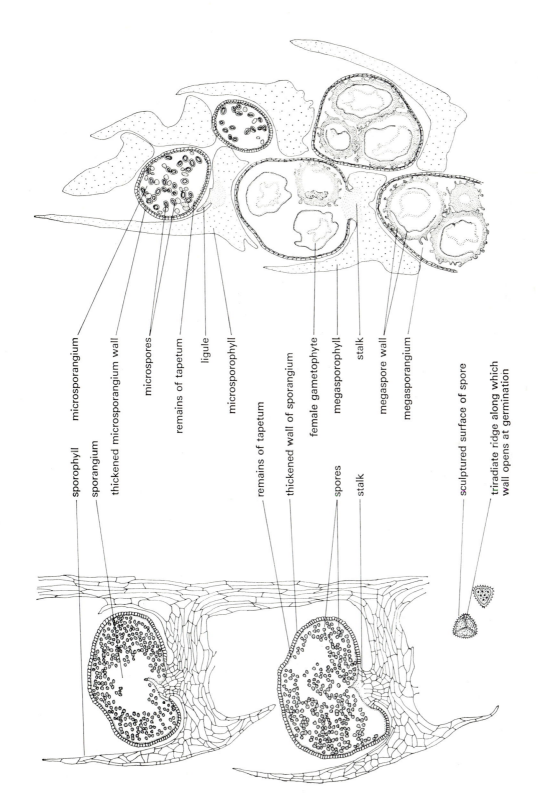

sporophyll

sporangium

thickened microsporangium wall

remains of tapetum

thickened wall of sporangium

spores

stalk

sculptured surface of spore

triradiate ridge along which
wall opens at germination

Drawing of Specimen 113

microsporangium

microspores

remains of tapetum

ligule

microsporophyll

female gametophyte

megasporophyll

stalk

megaspore wall

megasporangium

Drawing of Specimen 114

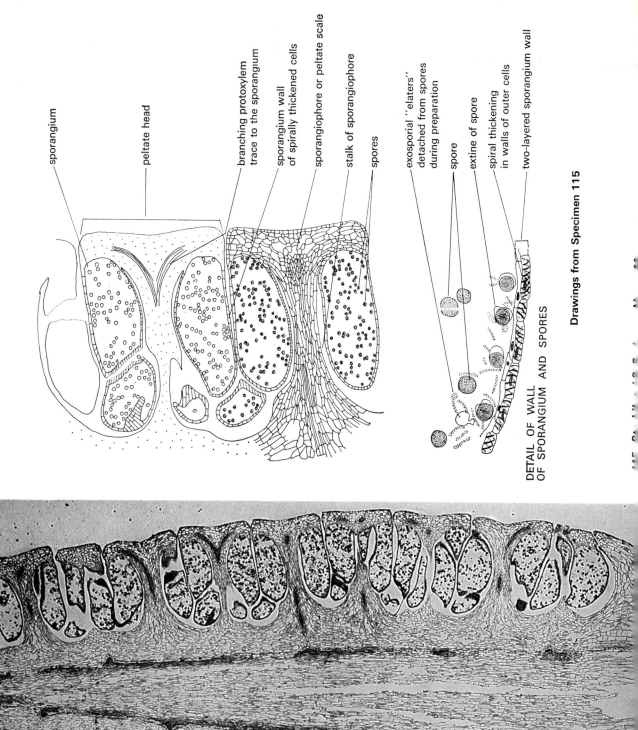

sporangium

peltate head

branching protoxylem trace to the sporangium

sporangium wall of spirally thickened cells

sporangiophore or peltate scale

stalk of sporangiophore

spores

exosporial "elaters" detached from spores during preparation

spore

extine of spore

spiral thickening in walls of outer cells

two-layered sporangium wall

DETAIL OF WALL
OF SPORANGIUM AND SPORES

Drawings from Specimen 115

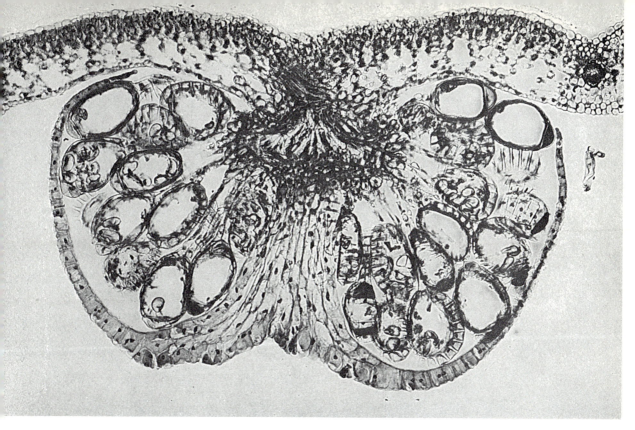

116. **Sorus,** LS, *Dryopteris.* Mag. ×200

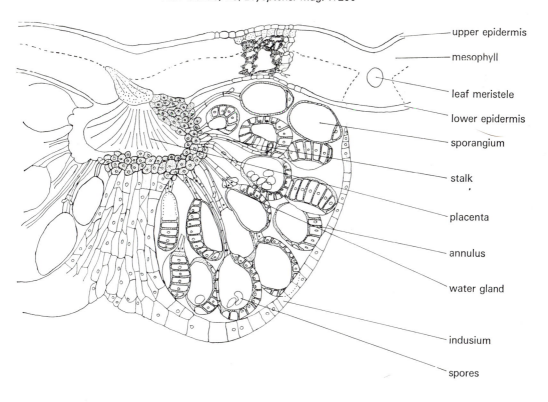

upper epidermis

mesophyll

leaf meristele

lower epidermis

sporangium

stalk

placenta

annulus

water gland

indusium

spores

Drawing of Specimen 116

117. Sporangium, LS, *Dryopteris.* Mag. ×450

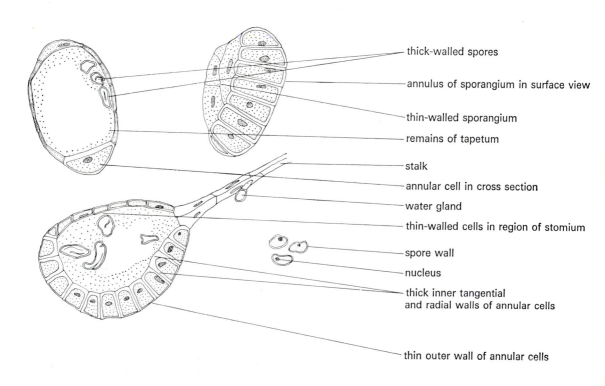

thick-walled spores

annulus of sporangium in surface view

thin-walled sporangium

remains of tapetum

stalk

annular cell in cross section

water gland

thin-walled cells in region of stomium

spore wall

nucleus

thick inner tangential
and radial walls of annular cells

thin outer wall of annular cells

Drawings from Specimen 117

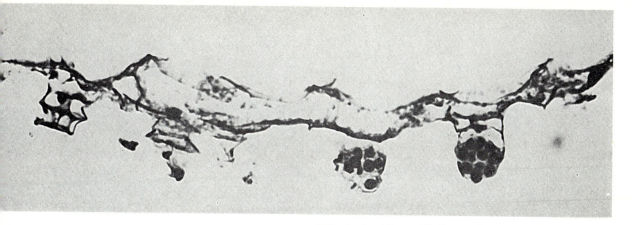

118. **Antheridium,** LS, *Dryopteris.* Mag. ×550

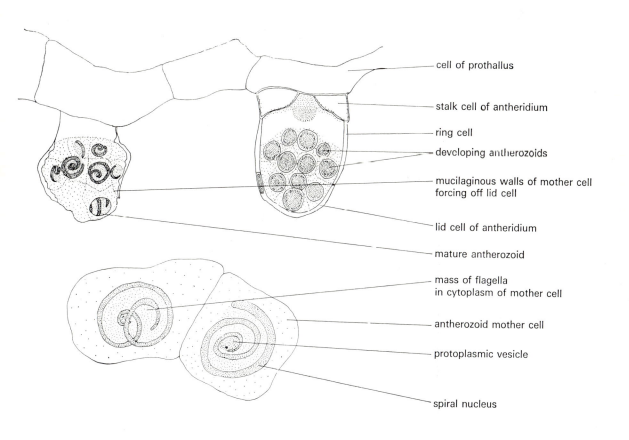

cell of prothallus

stalk cell of antheridium

ring cell

developing antherozoids

mucilaginous walls of mother cell
forcing off lid cell

lid cell of antheridium

mature antherozoid

mass of flagella
in cytoplasm of mother cell

antherozoid mother cell

protoplasmic vesicle

spiral nucleus

Drawing of Specimen 118

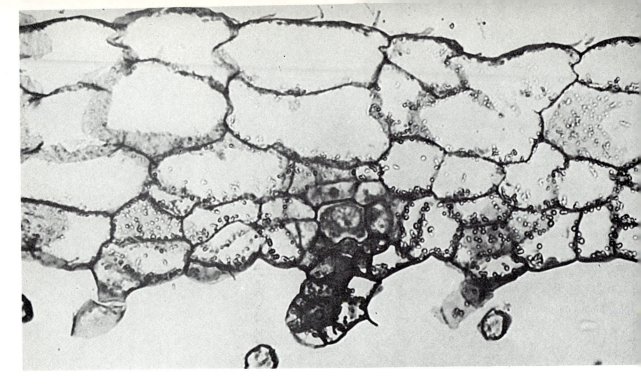

119. **Archegonium,** LS, *Dryopteris* Mag. ×650

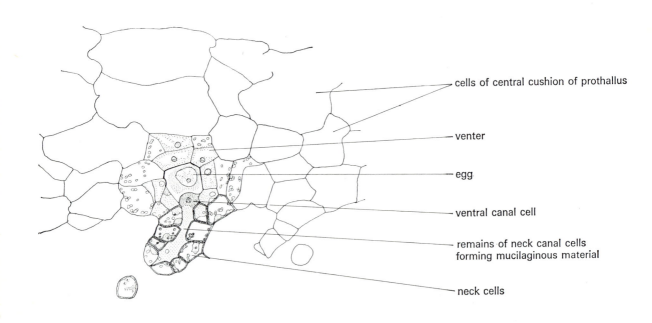

cells of central cushion of prothallus

venter

egg

ventral canal cell

remains of neck canal cells forming mucilaginous material

neck cells

Drawing of Specimen 119

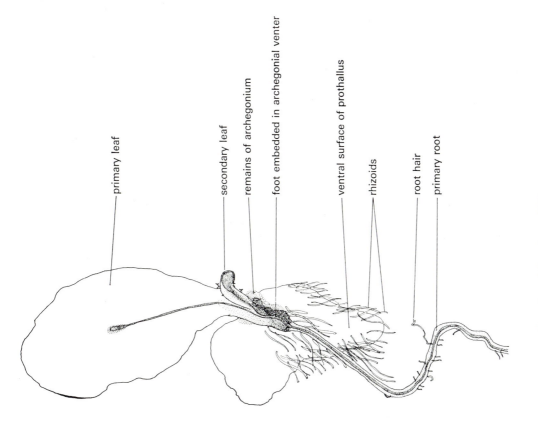

primary leaf

secondary leaf

remains of archegonium

foot embedded in archegonial venter

ventral surface of prothallus

rhizoids

root hair

primary root

Drawing of Specimen 120

120. **Sporophyte,** E, *Dryopteris*. Mag. ×10

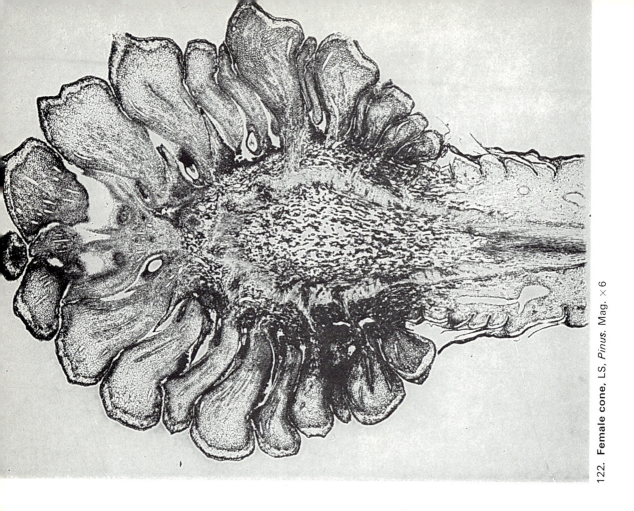

122. **Female cone**, LS, *Pinus*. Mag. ×6

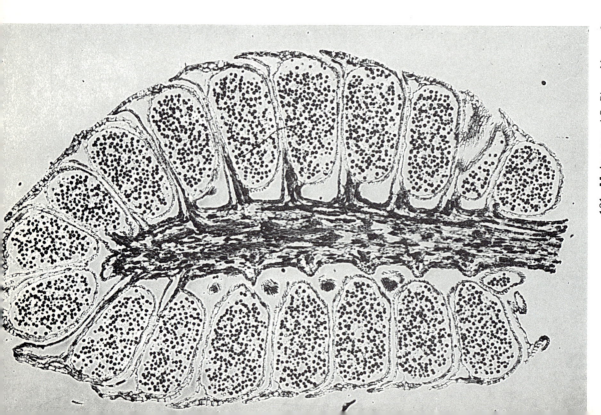

121. **Male cone**, LS, *Pinus*. Mag. ×9

microsporophyll

microsporangium

microspores (pollen grains)

axis of cone

woody ovuliferous scale

cone axis

vascular trace

bract scale

wall of microsporangium

pollen grains

integument

nucellus or megasporangium

air sac

intine

megaspore mother cell

antheridial or generative cell

tube cell

pollen grain with pollen tube

thickened wall

micropyle

DETAIL OF MEGASPORANGIUM

Drawing of Specimen 122

Drawing of Specimen 121

DETAIL OF WALL OF MICROSPORANGIUM
AND POLLEN GRAINS

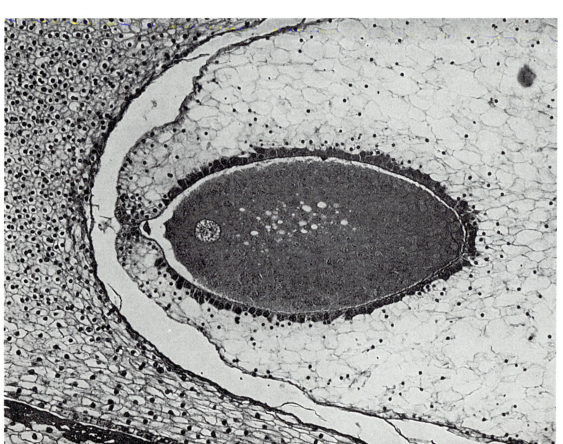

123. **Archegonium**, LS, *Pinus*. Mag. × 65

124. **Ovule at fertilisation**, LS, *Pinus*. Mag. × 75

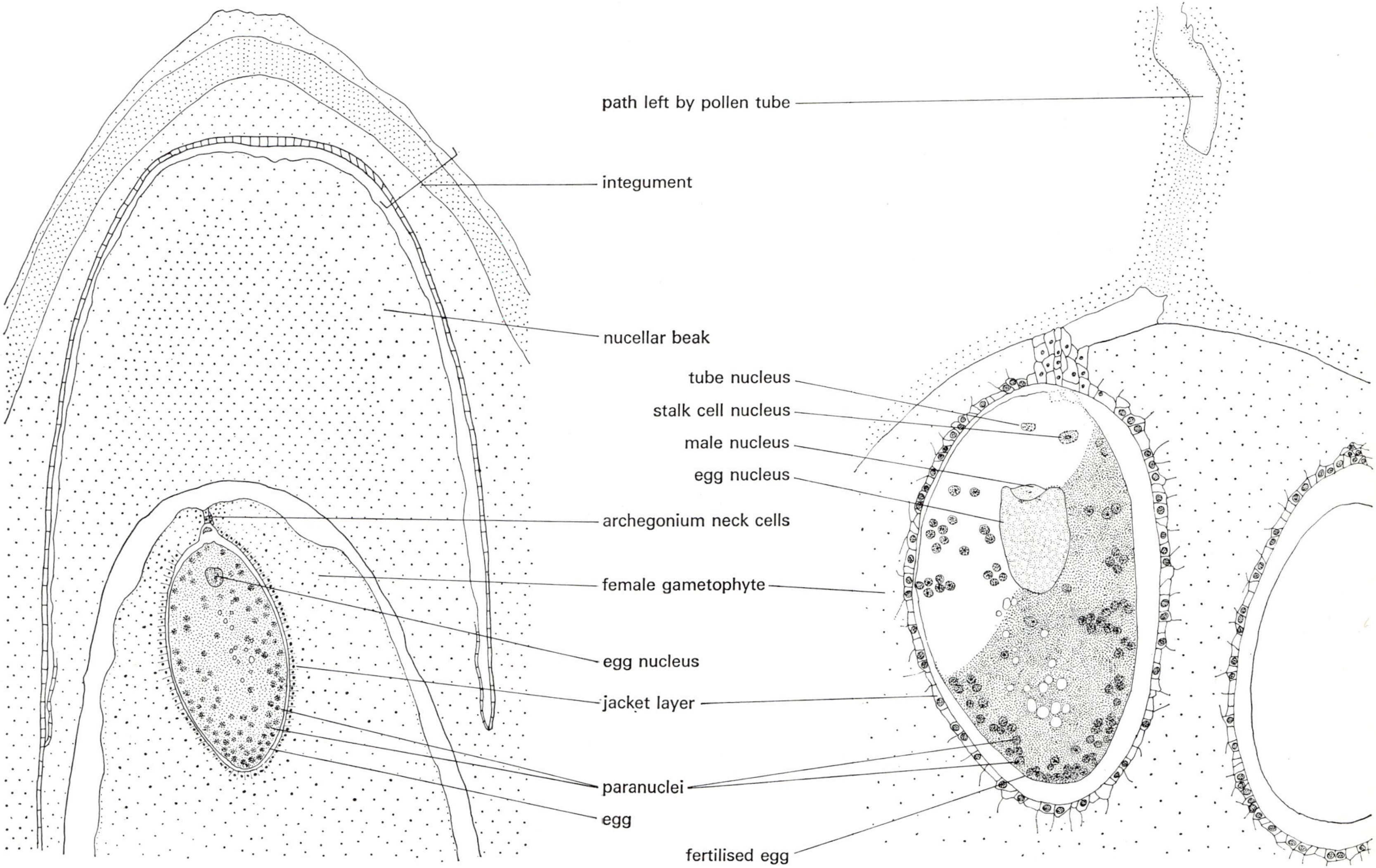

path left by pollen tube

integument

nucellar beak

tube nucleus

stalk cell nucleus

male nucleus

egg nucleus

archegonium neck cells

female gametophyte

egg nucleus

jacket layer

paranuclei

egg

fertilised egg

Drawing of Specimen 124

Drawing of Specimen 123

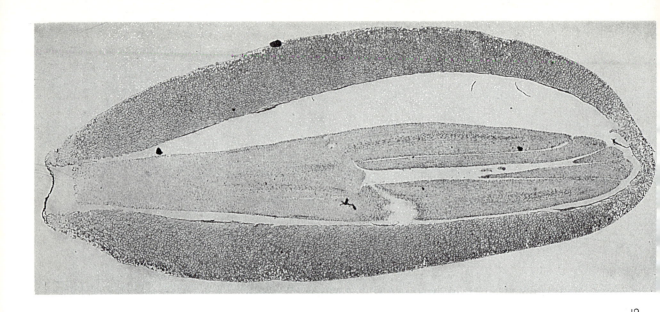

126. **Embryo**, LS, *Pinus*. Mag. ×15

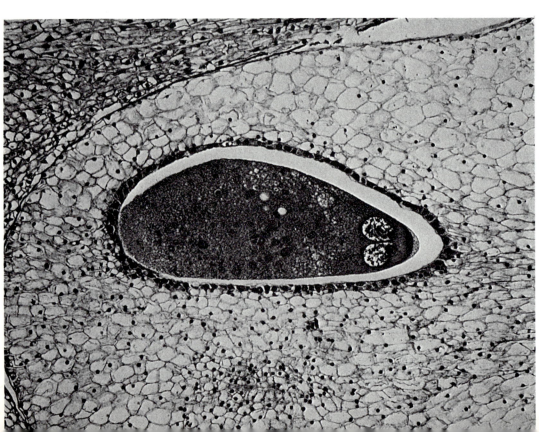

125. **Proembryo**, LS, *Pinus*. Mag. ×120

104

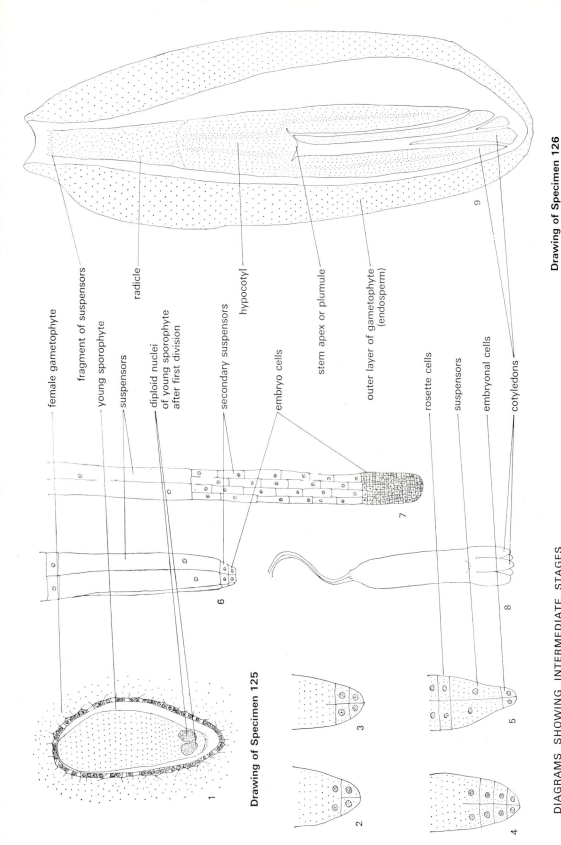

female gametophyte

fragment of suspensors

young sporophyte

suspensors

diploid nuclei
of young sporophyte
after first division

secondary suspensors

hypocotyl

embryo cells

stem apex or plumule

outer layer of gametophyte
(endosperm)

radicle

rosette cells

suspensors

embryonal cells

cotyledons

Drawing of Specimen 125

Drawing of Specimen 126

1

2

3

4

5

6

7

8

9

DIAGRAMS SHOWING INTERMEDIATE STAGES
IN EMBRYO DEVELOPMENT

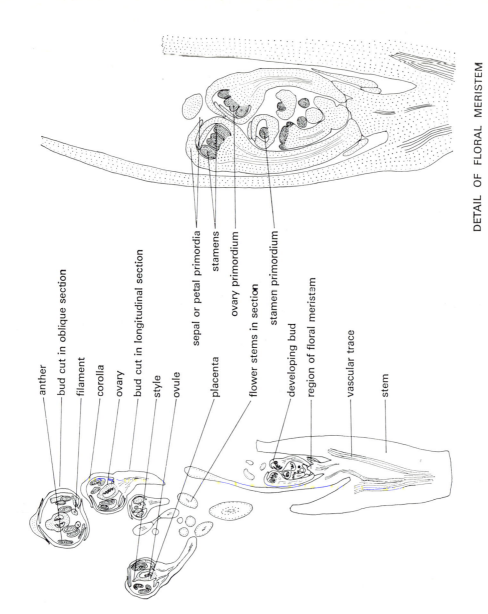

DETAIL OF FLORAL MERISTEM

sepal or petal primordia
stamens
ovary primordium
stamen primordium

anther
bud cut in oblique section
filament
corolla
ovary
bud cut in longitudinal section
style
ovule

placenta

flower stems in section

developing bud
region of floral meristem

vascular trace

stem

Drawing of Specimen 127

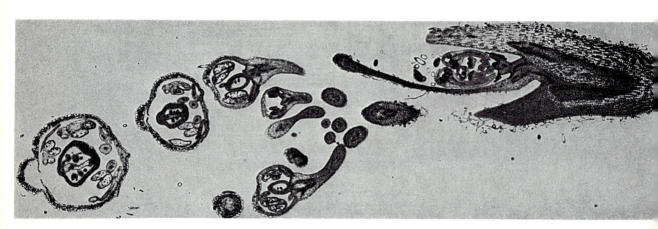

127. **Floral tip,** LS, *Capsella*. Mag. ×20

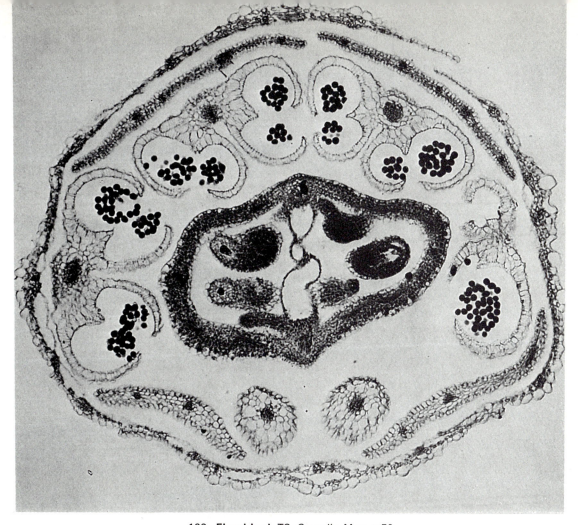

128. **Floral bud**, TS, *Capsella*. Mag. ×50

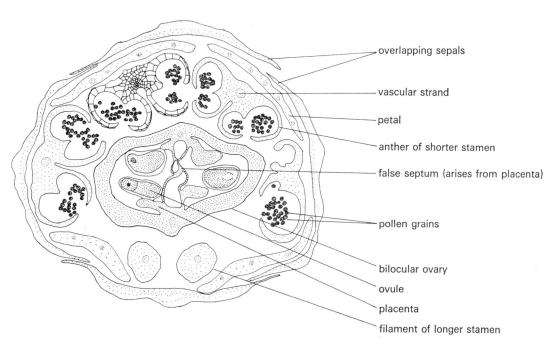

overlapping sepals

vascular strand

petal

anther of shorter stamen

false septum (arises from placenta)

pollen grains

bilocular ovary

ovule

placenta

filament of longer stamen

Drawing of Specimen 128

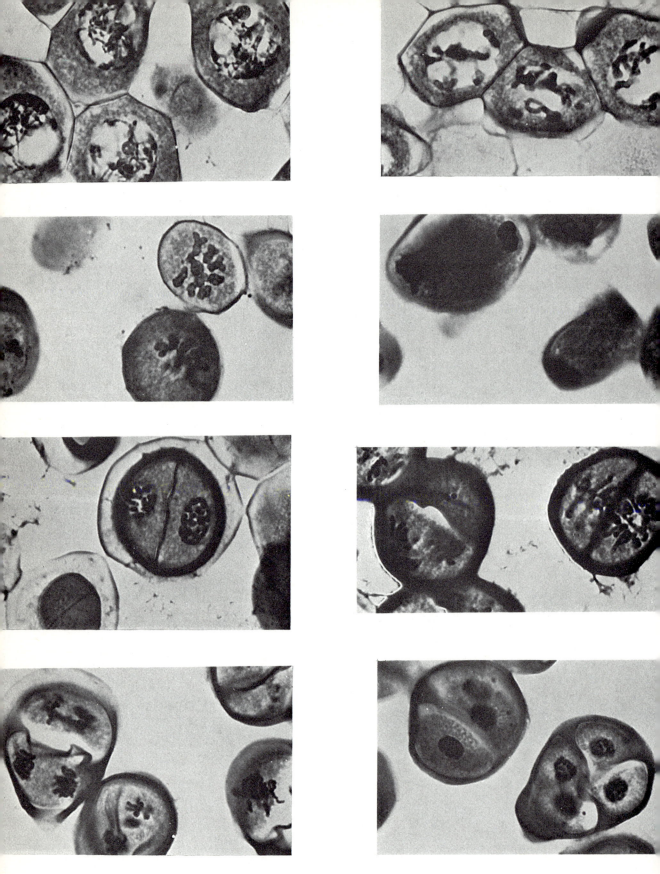

129a. to h. **Anther,** TS, *Lilium,* for stages in meiosis. Mag. ×750

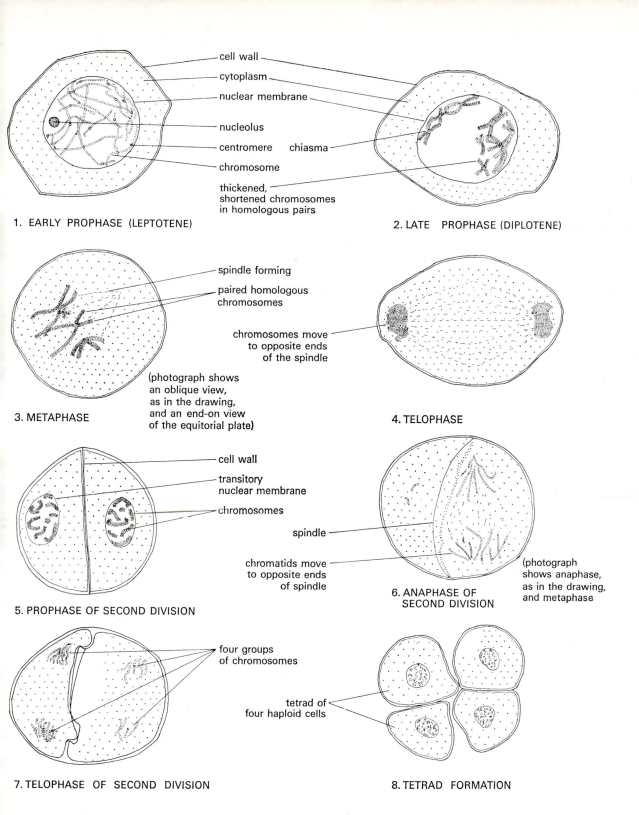

1. EARLY PROPHASE (LEPTOTENE)

cell wall
cytoplasm
nuclear membrane
nucleolus
centromere   chiasma
chromosome
thickened,
shortened chromosomes
in homologous pairs

2. LATE   PROPHASE (DIPLOTENE)

spindle forming
paired homologous
chromosomes

chromosomes move
to opposite ends
of the spindle

(photograph shows
an oblique view,
as in the drawing,
and an end-on view
of the equitorial plate)

3. METAPHASE

4. TELOPHASE

cell wall
transitory
nuclear membrane
chromosomes

spindle

chromatids move
to opposite ends
of spindle

5. PROPHASE OF SECOND DIVISION

6. ANAPHASE OF
SECOND DIVISION

(photograph
shows anaphase,
as in the drawing,
and metaphase

four groups
of chromosomes

tetrad of
four haploid cells

7. TELOPHASE OF SECOND DIVISION

8. TETRAD FORMATION

Drawings from Specimen 129 showing stages in meiosis

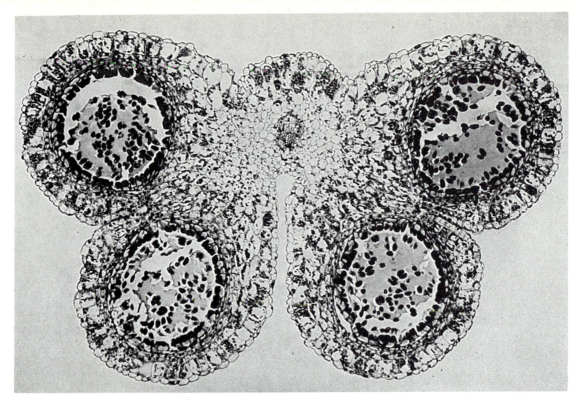

130. **Anther,** TS, *Lilium.* Mag. ×150

131. **Anther,** TS, dehisced, *Lilium.* Mag. ×150

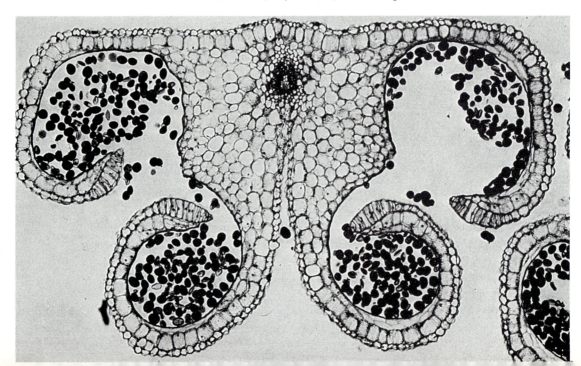

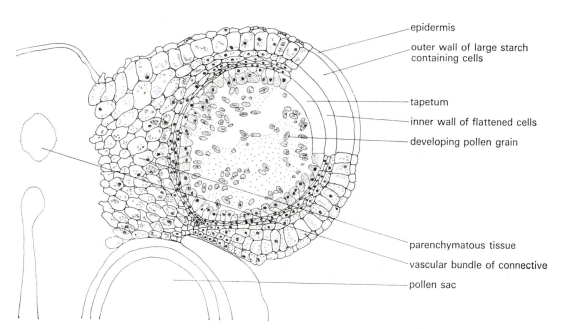

epidermis

outer wall of large starch
containing cells

tapetum

inner wall of flattened cells

developing pollen grain

parenchymatous tissue

vascular bundle of connective

pollen sac

Drawing of Specimen 130

exine

generative nucleus

pollen grain

tube nucleus

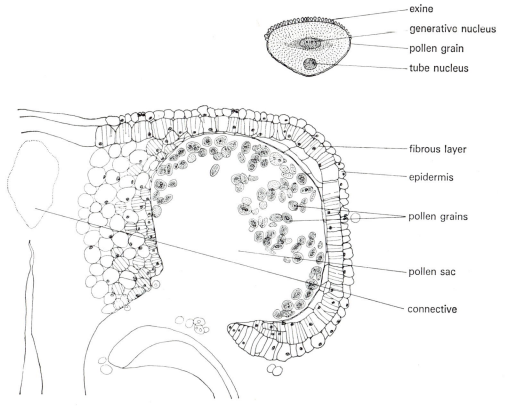

fibrous layer

epidermis

pollen grains

pollen sac

connective

Drawing of Specimen 131

LILIUM EMBRYO SAC DEVELOPMENT

Lilium is usually used to illustrate embryo sac development but differs from the normal type of development.

The following diagrams show these differences —

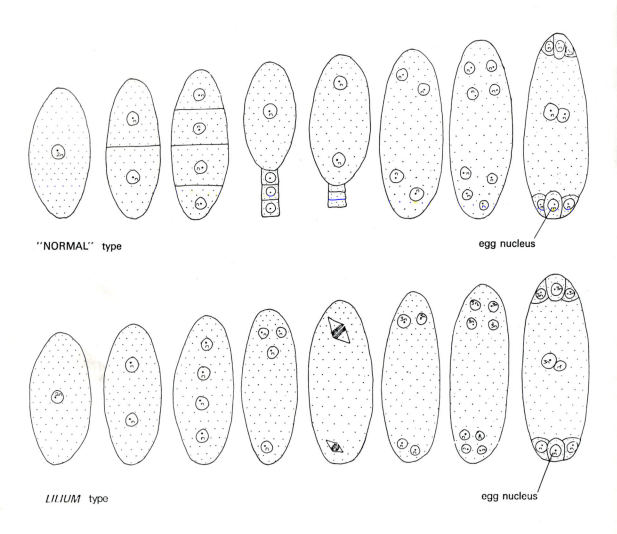

"NORMAL" type

egg nucleus

LILIUM type

egg nucleus

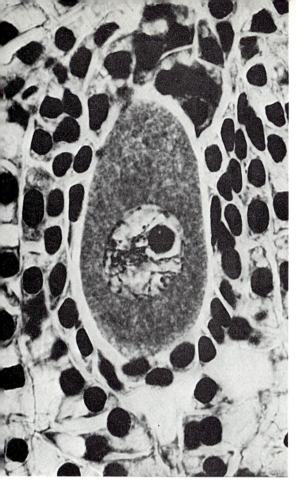

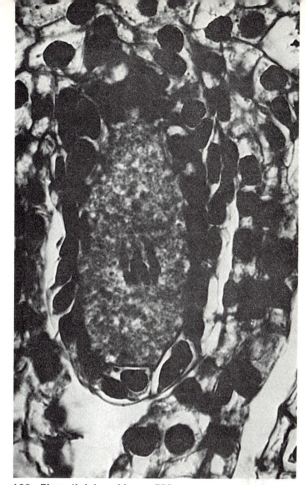

132. Uninucleate stage. Mag. ×550

133. First division. Mag. ×550

LILIUM EMBRYO-SAC DEVELOPMENT

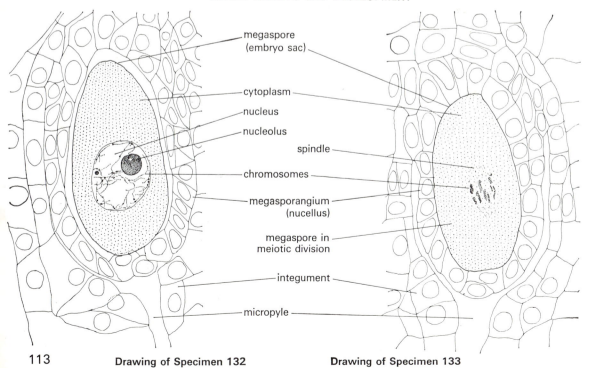

megaspore
(embryo sac)

cytoplasm

nucleus

nucleolus

spindle

chromosomes

megasporangium
(nucellus)

megaspore in
meiotic division

integument

micropyle

113   **Drawing of Specimen 132**   **Drawing of Specimen 133**

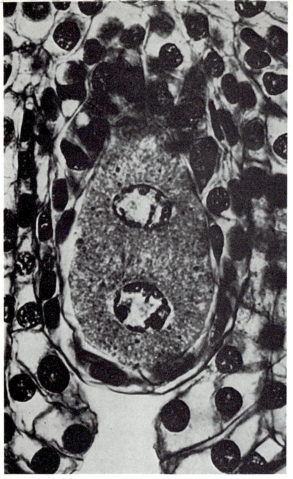

134. First two-nucleate stage. Mag. ×550

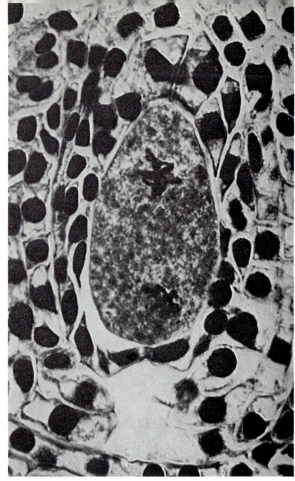

135. Second division. Mag. ×550

LILIUM EMBRYO-SAC DEVELOPMENT

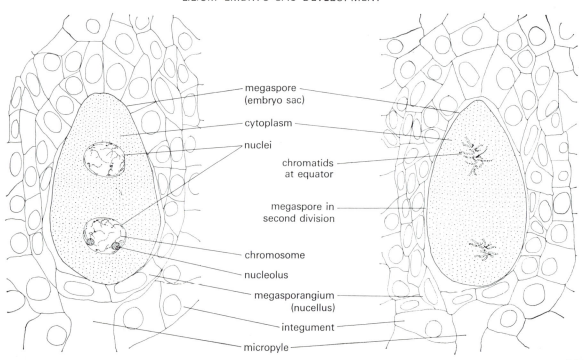

megaspore (embryo sac)

cytoplasm

nuclei

chromatids at equator

megaspore in second division

chromosome

nucleolus

megasporangium (nucellus)

integument

micropyle

Drawing of Specimen 134

Drawing of Specimen 135

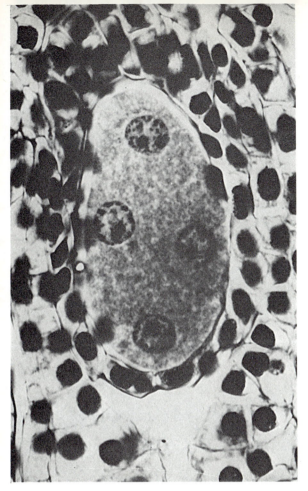

136. **First four-nucleate stage.** Mag. ×550

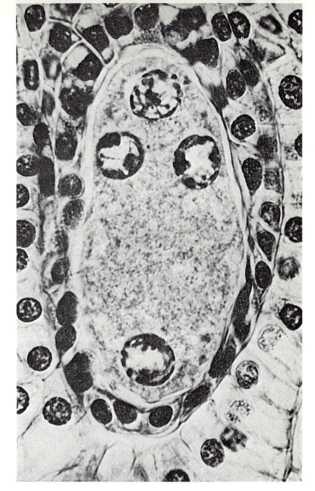

137. **Migration of three nuclei.** Mag. ×550

LILIUM EMBRYO-SAC DEVELOPMENT

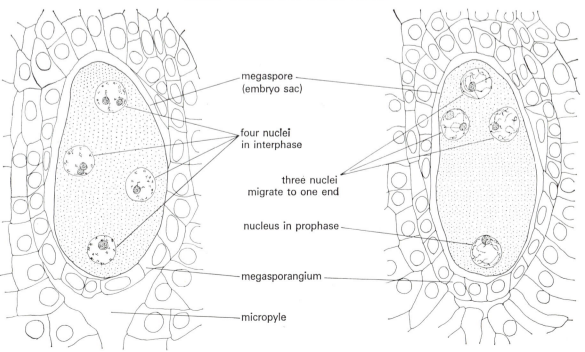

megaspore
(embryo sac)

four nuclei
in interphase

three nuclei
migrate to one end

nucleus in prophase

megasporangium

micropyle

Drawing of Specimen 136   **Drawing of Specimen 137**

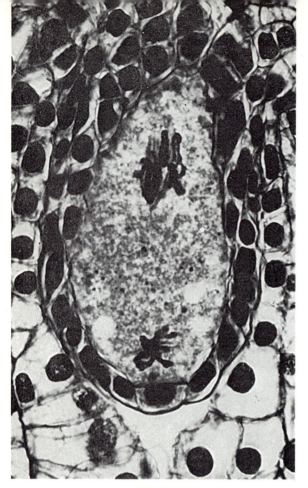

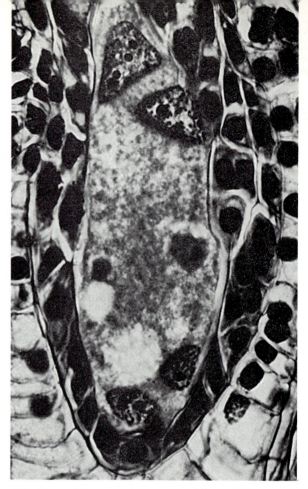

138. Third division. Mag. ×550

139. Second four-nucleate stage. Mag. ×550

LILIUM EMBRYO-SAC DEVELOPMENT

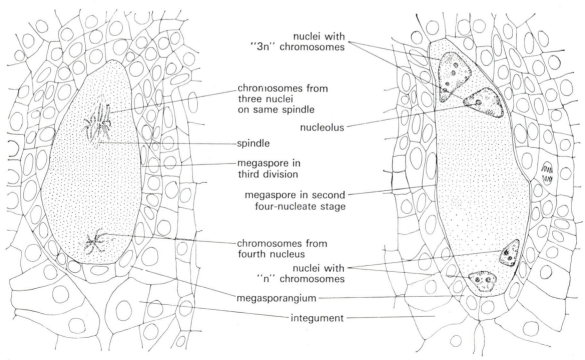

nuclei with "3n" chromosomes

chromosomes from three nuclei on same spindle

nucleolus

spindle

megaspore in third division

megaspore in second four-nucleate stage

chromosomes from fourth nucleus

nuclei with "n" chromosomes

megasporangium

integument

Drawing of Specimen 138

Drawing of Specimen 139

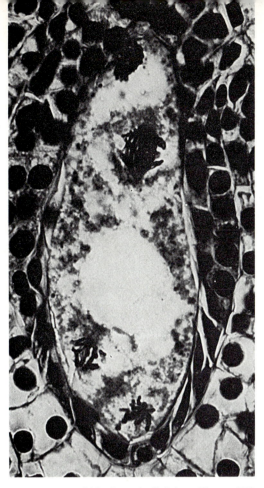

140. Fourth division. Mag. ×550

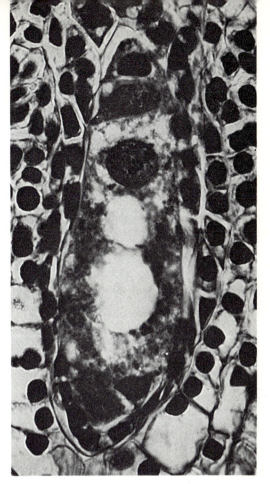

141. Immature female gametophyte. Mag. ×450

LILIUM EMBRO-SAC DEVELOPMENT

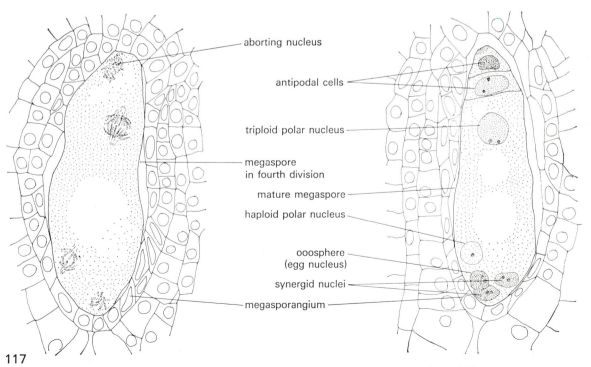

aborting nucleus

antipodal cells

triploid polar nucleus

megaspore
in fourth division

mature megaspore

haploid polar nucleus

ooosphere
(egg nucleus)

synergid nuclei

megasporangium

Drawing of Specimen 140

Drawing of Specimen 141

117

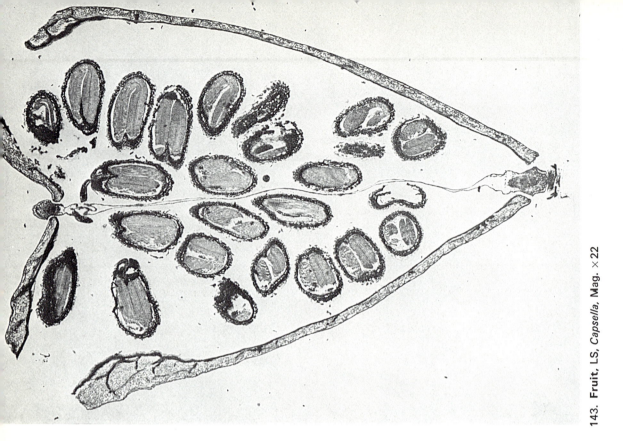

143. **Fruit**, LS, *Capsella*. Mag. × 22

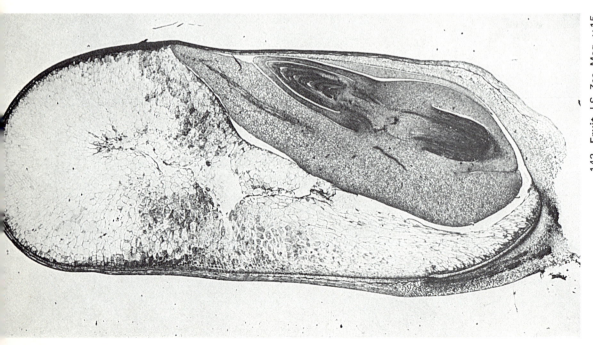

142. **Fruit**, LS *Zea*. Mag. ×15

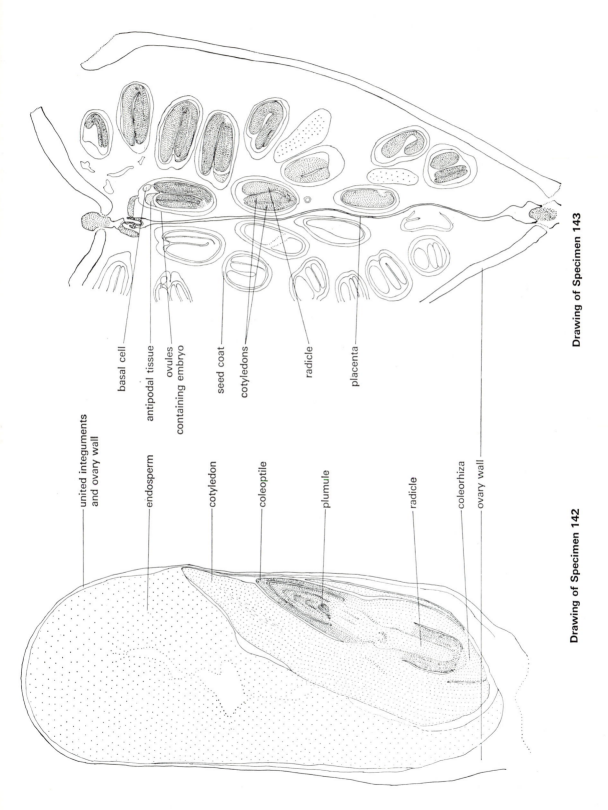

basal cell

antipodal tissue

ovules
containing embryo

seed coat

cotyledons

radicle

placenta

Drawing of Specimen 143

united integuments
and ovary wall

endosperm

cotyledon

coleoptile

plumule

radicle

coleorhiza

ovary wall

Drawing of Specimen 142

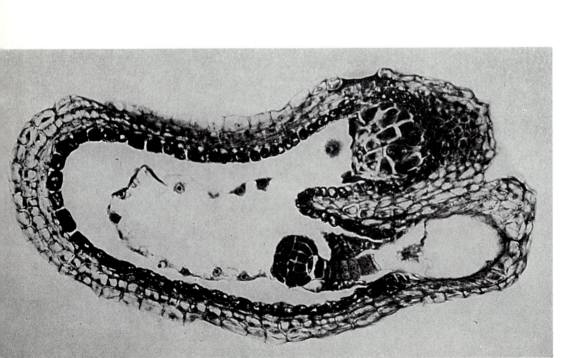

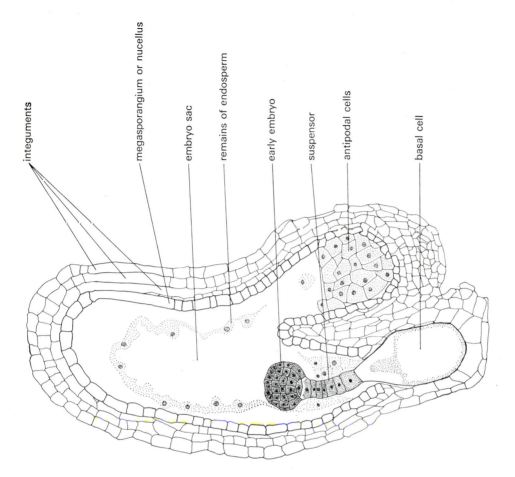

integuments

megasporangium or nucellus

embryo sac

remains of endosperm

early embryo

suspensor

antipodal cells

basal cell

Drawing of Specimen 144

CAPSELLA EMBRYOGENY

144. Early embryo, LS. Mag. ×300

145. **Differentiation of embryo, LS. Mag. ×750**

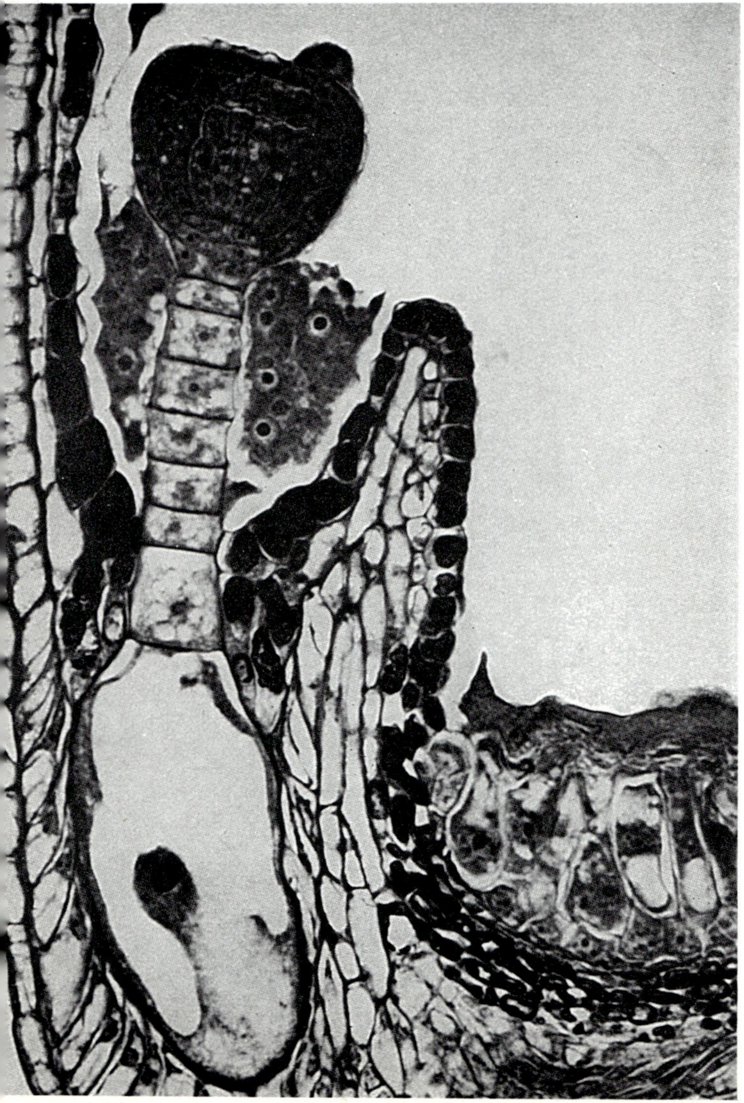

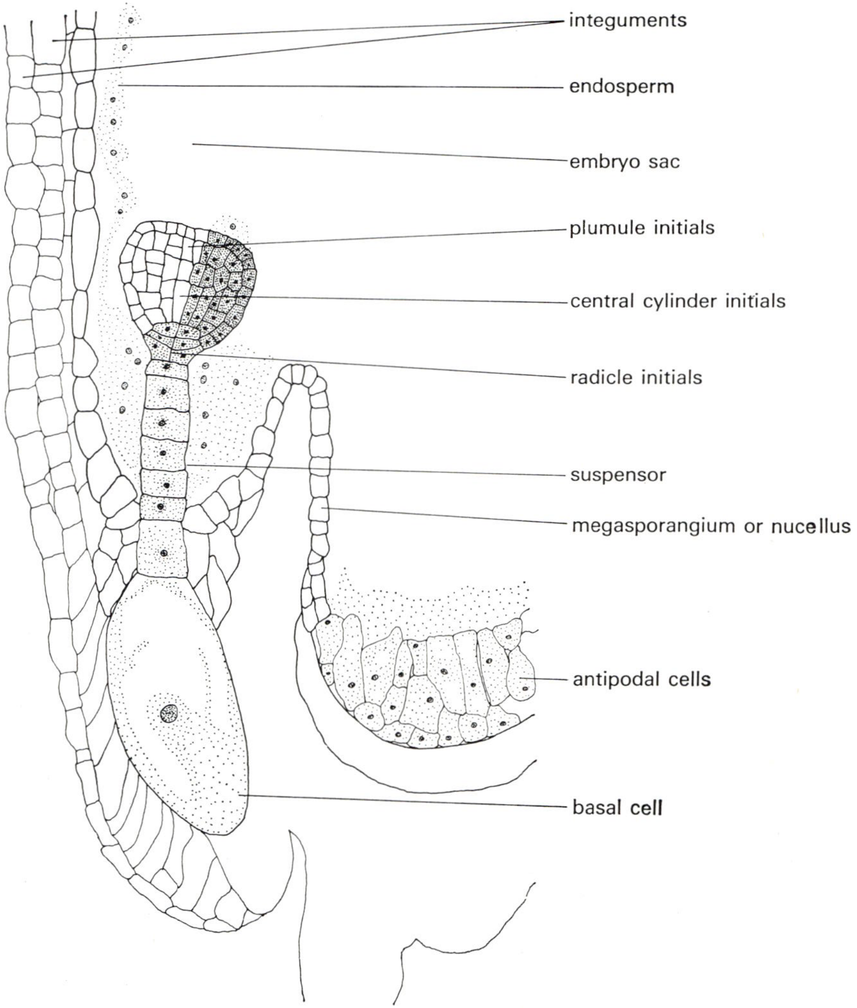

Drawing of Specimen 145

integuments

endosperm

embryo sac

plumule initials

central cylinder initials

radicle initials

suspensor

megasporangium or nucellus

antipodal cells

basal cell

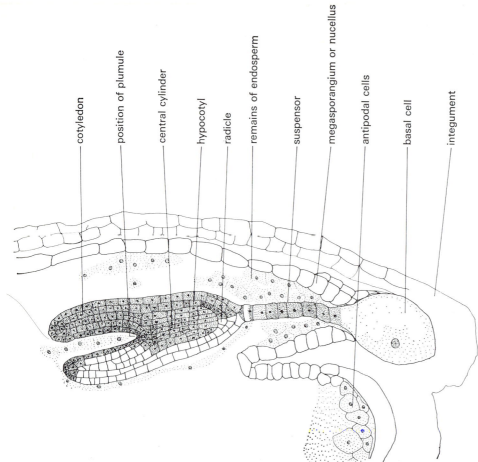

cotyledon

position of plumule

central cylinder

hypocotyl

radicle

remains of endosperm

suspensor

megasporangium or nucellus

antipodal cells

basal cell

integument

Drawing of Specimen 146

CAPSELLA EMBRYOGENY

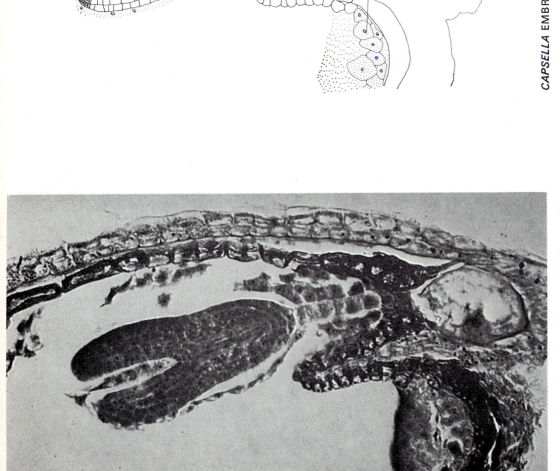

146. **Development of cotyledons, LS. Mag. × 450**

147. Well-differentiated embryo, LS. Mag. ×200

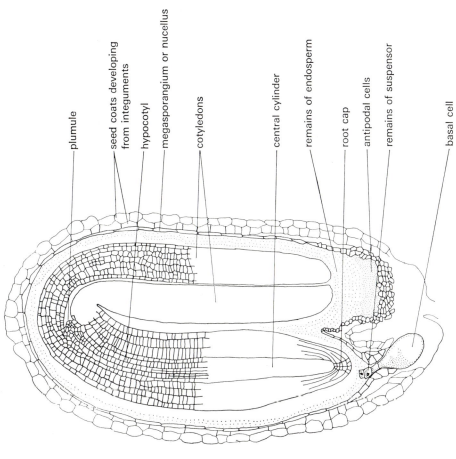

plumule

seed coats developing
from integuments

hypocotyl

megasporangium or nucellus

cotyledons

central cylinder

remains of endosperm

root cap

antipodal cells

remains of suspensor

basal cell

Drawing of Specimen 147

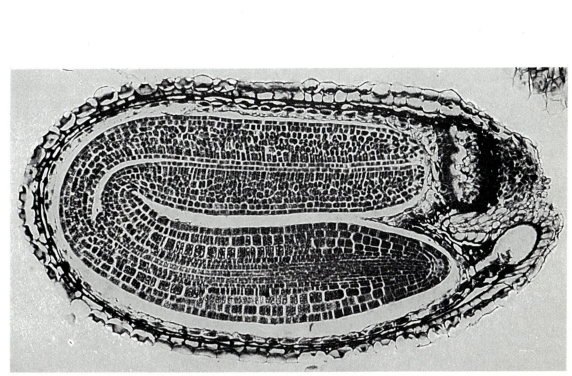